I SEE YOU - A WOMAN WHO DARED TO BE SEEN

How One Man Hepled Me See Myself Again

Katarzyna Laskowska

Feather & Fire Publishing

Feather & Fire

A Letter to Christopher
My love...
I don't even know where to begin.
Maybe with this — if it weren't for you, this book wouldn't exist.
I wouldn't have written it. I wouldn't have had the strength. Or the reason.
Because before you came... I didn't believe in anything anymore.
Certainly not in the possibility that someone like you could be real.
And yet, you arrived. Quietly. Without declarations. Without games.
And you stayed.
You didn't try to fix me. You didn't teach me how to live.
You didn't try to make me better.
You just were.
And for the first time, I could just be with someone.
With all my mess, all my demons, the tenderness I was too scared to show.
With everything that had made others walk away.
But you didn't.
You saw me.
And I know I'm not easy.
I know I'm chaos. I have fears that come out of nowhere.
But with you, those fears... shrink.
Because I know you hold me — even when I fall apart.
Thank you for your hands — not just touching, but saying, "Don't be afraid."
For your eyes that see beyond my past.
For your silence that speaks more gently than a thousand words.
Thank you for every morning you've shared with me.
For the coffee. The kiss on the forehead. For being.
With no conditions. No control. No fear.
This book isn't about you.
But every page smells like you.
You are my safe harbor.
My truth. My light.
The one person with whom I don't have to be anyone but myself.
And I know you love me — exactly as I am.
Thank you for being my home.
And for teaching me, every single day, what love truly means.

Forever Yours,
Okruszek (your crumb of happiness)

I guess I'm old - fashioned...
I want to belong to just one man,
and hear him say - "You're mine"

K.L

From the Author

This book wasn't written at a desk.
It wasn't planned, outlined, or structured into a tidy narrative.
It poured out of me — out of pain, wonder, longing, and the sheer disbelief that such a connection could even exist.
Every chapter is a piece of the process.
Sometimes scribbled on my knee, sometimes at four in the morning, in the car, in a café, after a conversation, after a touch, after silence.
Sometimes after wrestling with demons screaming, "Run. It's too good to be real."
You know that feeling, when your head spins with a thousand thoughts, and they all want to come out at once?
I have ADHD.
And that's exactly how this book was born — chaotically, honestly, truthfully.
Some themes return. But each time, from a different angle. A different day. A different version of me, ready for a different truth.
I didn't want to force this into order.
Because love isn't a linear graph, and healing the soul doesn't follow a table of contents.
You may notice recurring thoughts, familiar words —
but if you look closer, each reflection carries a new weight, a new light, and a different kind of shadow.
This book is a soul map of a woman who, after walking through

fire, is slowly learning to see.
Herself. Him. And the truth between them.
Don't expect structure.
Expect truth.
And let it speak to you, too.
With love,
Katarzyna Laskowska

———————————————————————

❧ ABOUT ME

This isn't my first book.
It's the second part of the story of the woman you can't forget.
If this is the first one you're holding in your hands — good.
But if you really want to understand who I am now, you might want to go back.
Back to the one written in pain, in ashes, in pieces.
That's where you'll find everything that fell apart in me.
Here — you'll find everything that started to come back together.
I won't go into details.
Long story short: I was shattered. And I put myself back together.
Today, I'm a woman who sees the world differently than I used to.

Not because life got easier — but because I stopped lying to myself.
I still have moments when my demons catch up with me.
But I'm not afraid of them anymore.

Because I know now — if you meet someone who doesn't run from your wounds,
you can finally breathe for real.

This isn't some sugar-coated love story.
It's a story about the fact that even if life has been completely fucked up —
you can still find real love.
Not a fairytale.
Love.
Real.
The kind that doesn't hurt. Doesn't run. Doesn't manipulate.

I'm writing this part as a woman who knows who she is.
Who's been through her own hell — and isn't ashamed of it.
Who doesn't want to be "nice" anymore — just real.

Don't give up. Ever.
Don't listen to anyone who tells you it's "too late" or "not possible."
It is.

It'll be fucking hard.
But that's exactly why it's worth it.

Because when something real finally comes along —
you know you're alive. Fully.

And that it all makes sense.

Author's Note:
They told us to be sweet, small, and silent.
And look what it cost us.
Now watch what happens when we stop listening.

🐦 THOSE TEARS WERE WORTH THE SPARKS IN MY EYES

Four years ago, I died.
I needed that death to rise from the ashes.
To be reborn — not as someone stronger,
but as someone truer.
Not more resistant — but more awake.

The energy of death is ruthless, raw, relentless…
but it's also cleansing.
That day, I buried my former self.

The values that weren't mine.
The masks that had fused with my skin.
The roles I played because I was told I should.

Aga Sun awakened.
Not as a new version —
but as Me.
The real one.

I walked through fire.
Through hell.
Through a silence so thick it hurt.
But I walked.
And that's when a new era began.

It wasn't just change.
It was a return.
To my inner truth.
To the soul I had once lost.

The Queen of Swords became the Empress.
And now... she is becoming the High Priestess.

My femininity was tested in flames.
It was suffocated, silenced, tamed —
until it learned how to burn without destroying.

Now I know who I am.
And I know I am safe.
My heart chakra is healed.
This is my triumph.
My quiet miracle.

Remember this:

What broke you wasn't meant to destroy you.
It came so you could rebuild — this time on your own terms.
Your weakness is not failure.
It's the foundation of a new kind of strength.

Despair is purification.
When you hit rock bottom,

at least you finally have something solid to push off from.
And when you do — don't look back.
Go.
And do it to spite the pain,
to spite those who didn't believe in you.

Get up.
Stand tall.
Adjust your crown.
Step into your hard mode.

And you'll see...
The doors will open.
The horizon will expand.
And one day, you'll look back and say:
"I had no idea everything would fall into place so beautifully."

Trust yourself.
Stay with yourself.
Win yourself.

If I did it — so can you.

This is the journey from hell to heaven.
It was heavy.
I stumbled.
I crawled.
But I kept moving — toward the light.

And eventually, I stood up.
And now?
Now, I fly.

Every tear I shed,
every heartache,
every "I can't take this anymore" —
was worth these sparks in my eyes today.
My peace.
My joy.

And you know what?

Today, I know that what I lost…
was never real.
Because what I gained
is beyond anything I could've imagined.

If I could go back in time —
I wouldn't change a thing.

Because it was the best thing
that could've ever happened to me.

I'm grateful I let it all go.
That I didn't force the fight.
Even though, at the time,
I wanted to stop breathing.

Today, I breathe fully.
I savor life.
I look forward to every new day.

And I'm no longer afraid of death.
Because I know now —
sometimes it's just the beginning.

Author's Note:
Some women fall apart and stay shattered.
Others fall apart… and rise as fucking phoenixes.
Choose which one you want to be.

🌑 *When You're Ready, My Witch*🌑

by Jason Lapointe

When you're ready, my Witch,
choose well the Man who will walk beside you.
Choose the one who, if needed, will take you to the
ends of the Earth…

The one for whom distance and space mean
nothing when it comes to being with you.
Choose the one who will wait patiently when you
lose yourself in your paths of darkness.
Choose the one who is strong and grounded,
the one who will bring you back when
you're too lost to find your way.

Choose the one who believes in you when you no
longer believe in anything.
The one who has seen the full scope of your
potential — and wasn't afraid.
The one who has measured the depths of your
madness — and loved you even more.
Choose the one who is strong enough not to feel
threatened by your power.
The one who can stand beside you without
flinching.
The one who isn't afraid of the fire burning in your
belly.
The one who isn't scared of your gifts.

Choose the wolf. The warrior.
Because it takes a powerful man to walk beside a
wild woman.
You need a man who can brush shoulders
with light — and not get burned.

But most of all,
choose the one who will never give up.
Never.

🐾 FOUR WORDS.

Four Elements.

Four Essences of Energy

Stone – earth.
Foundation. Stability. Presence.
A man who stands firmly on his feet doesn't disappear. He doesn't run.
He's there. He doesn't shine. He doesn't perform.
But you can lean on him like a rock that survives every storm.
Silk – water.

Softness. Depth. Tenderness.
His emotions don't explode — they flow.
Like a stream that moves slowly, but reaches deep.
He can hold you with a look, calm you with a word, stay close — without overwhelming.

Feather – air.
Intuition. Thoughts. Freedom.
Your words, carrying meaning.
Your lightness that keeps you afloat.
Your doubts, your questions, your mind that never stops searching.
Your soul that's been flying for years, looking for a safe place to land.

Fire – fire.
Strength. Truth. Passion.
Your anger, your tears, your emotions burning through every cell of your body.
You are fire — the kind that doesn't tolerate pretending.
The kind that burns through lies.
The kind that screams:
Give me real life. Not a fake connection.

🐚 SOUL LOVE DOESN'T MAKE NOISE.

It Comes as a Whisper.

I t arrives quietly. Almost imperceptibly. Without fireworks or grand declarations. It doesn't cut through the air riding a white horse, nor does it strike the heart like a bolt of lightning. It's more like a breath—deep, familiar—the kind you suddenly feel beside your own. And you just know.

Soul love doesn't need a performance. It doesn't crave attention —it *resonates*. It stirs something inside you that's been silent for lifetimes. You know instantly that this is not by chance. It's not a flirtation, not infatuation, not a projection of your unmet needs. It's something greater. Something that existed long before you ever learned to say "I love you."

It doesn't look like a fairytale. It doesn't smell like Disney. It doesn't sparkle like a rom-com. This is love for kings and queens. For souls who have lived through hell. Who remember the scent of blood, the silence after betrayal, the ashes of things that were meant to last. This is love for those who no longer seek salvation —because they've already saved themselves. For those who don't want to be rescued—they want to be *real*.

He doesn't need to save you. You no longer need to defend yourself. Because this love doesn't threaten. It doesn't want to possess. It *sees*. It sees all of you—your shadows, the lines around your eyes, the weight you've carried since childhood. And it says: *I'm here. You don't have to prove anything anymore.*

This is love for those who recognize each other not by face, but by *frequency*. Who remember each other from past lives, even if they never say it aloud. Who feel at home in a touch, and hear entire conversations in silence.

This is the meeting of the divine feminine and the divine masculine. Two poles. Two energies that don't try to dominate —but to *dance together*. As if they've been rehearsing this one sacred movement their whole lives.

And when the dance begins, you can't stop it. Because it doesn't come from this world. It's a calling. A *remembering*. It's the soul whispering: *It's you. Finally.*

You no longer fear your softness. You're not ashamed of your tears. You don't pretend you don't long for someone. You don't play games. You simply *are*—bare, true, stripped of masks. And for the first time... you are truly *seen*. Not with the eyes. But with the soul.

This is not a love you can cage. It demands freedom. To grow. To breathe. To choose each other every single day—not out of fear of loneliness, but from a place of *deep, spiritual knowing.*

If this ever finds you—don't fuck it up. Don't run. Because love like this doesn't show up twice in one lifetime. And sometimes… not even in a dozen.

🐾 ONE DAY, HE WILL COME

One day, you'll meet someone
who won't flinch at your past.
He won't retreat from your pain,
won't be afraid of your scars,
won't run when he sees your tears.
He'll step closer.
He'll see it all—the broken pieces you've been gathering for years
—
and he won't hesitate to say:
"You don't have to fight alone anymore."

That day will come,
when, for the first time, you'll feel like you can lean in—
not because you're weak,
but because someone finally stands beside you, just as strong.

Someone who won't try to change you.
Who won't compete with you.
Who won't punish you for being exactly who you are.

He will see you.
As you are.
And love you... just like that.

That will be the moment you realize
that everything you went through,
every illusion of love you believed in,
was just the prelude to one real melody.

He will be the reason
you no longer doubt love is possible.
With him, you'll finally feel what it's like
to be important—without proving it.
To be loved—without struggling.
To be wanted—without playing games.

And one quiet day, when you look into his eyes,
with no grand speeches, no theatrics,
you'll say silently:

*"Real men do exist.
And I'm lucky enough... to be with one of them."*

And you'll understand something more.

It won't just be a beautiful day.
It will be the beginning of a new life.

Yours.
His.
Both of yours.

Author's Note

Don't lose faith just because you've waited too long.

Sometimes life tests your patience before it gives you something sacred.

Don't fear a new beginning.

Sometimes it feels like the very first breath after drowning far too long.

🐾 IT'S
NOT LOVE.

IT'S A WOUND.

He walks into the room—and something inside you trembles.
You forget how to breathe.
Time stops.
Your heart races.
Your body tightens.

Your voice hides in your throat.
You think:
"This must be it. I've never felt chemistry like this before."

But your body remembers.
It remembers that hunger for attention.
That emptiness—when you waited as a little girl for someone to truly see you.
It remembers the longing for a touch that never came.
For a voice that was supposed to say, *"I see you. You matter."*

And now, when *he* enters your orbit,
your nervous system lights up like a battlefield:
"I know this! This might be the chance to finally get it!"

✧

It's not your heart falling in love.
It's your wound waking up.
It's your inner child—panicked and euphoric all at once—because he...
...looks at you the way no one ever did.
...touches you and you feel *alive, seen, wanted.*
And then disappears. Goes quiet. Sends that signal:
"Not yet."

So you find yourself right back in that same old place.
Waiting.
Tense.
Wondering what you have to *be* this time to be chosen.

✧

This is not love.
It's your sympathetic nervous system on high alert.
It's your inner child whispering:
*"I'll be good. I'll be quiet. I'll be beautiful. I'll be strong.
Just let me be enough this time."*

✧

Love doesn't come like an earthquake.
It doesn't set your nervous system on fire.

It doesn't hurt.
Love softens you.
Love lets you exhale.

Love is the person beside whom you can breathe.
The one who doesn't ask you to prove a damn thing.
The one whose presence makes your body say,
"I'm safe now."

So next time you feel that wild spark—
pause.
And ask yourself:
Is this love?
Or is it the echo of a girl still waiting for a miracle?

Author's Note

I know how easy it is to confuse the wound with love.
How loud your body can scream *"He's the one!"*
when it's really just your pain, rehearsing the same old play.
I know—because I've been there.
Because sometimes, I still end up there.

But here's what I've learned:
Real love doesn't tear your heart out.
It untangles the knots.
It doesn't need drama or sparks or fireworks.
It just needs truth.

And if those butterflies you feel seem too loud…
Maybe they're not butterflies.
Maybe they're a warning trying to fly away.
Hold yourself.
And keep walking.

Toward peace.
Toward love that doesn't hurt.

🐾 BEFORE YOU SAY YOU WANT LOVE...

Everyone says they want love.
That they're looking for closeness.
That they're ready for a relationship built on trust, honesty, and depth.

But... are they really?

How do you plan to build something true with another person when you're still chaos on the inside?

You carry wounds you've never even tried to face.
Childhood scars. The bitter taste of toxic love.
Unresolved anger toward your mother or father—stuffed down, not healed.
And then you wonder why you smother your partner, test them, hurt them, run…
or cling like a drowning man to a lifeboat.

You're not honest with yourself.
You pretend you don't care.
You act strong, like you've got it all under control.

But the truth is—you're afraid.
Afraid of your shadow.
Afraid of your softness.
Afraid of your need to be truly seen.

You don't know how to communicate.
You avoid hard conversations.
You either sweep things under the rug or go on the attack when someone touches your tender spots.
You think "communicating" means saying a lot.
It doesn't.
It means speaking honestly.
From the heart—not from the ego.

You don't have peace inside.
So how could you possibly build peace with someone else?

You can't really listen.
Your mind is always speaking over everything.
You're assertive only when you need to prove your point.
But when it's time to pause, to receive, to truly hear… you disappear.

You mock spirituality, silence, astrology, energy—because you're scared.
Because it's easier to laugh at the planets than admit you have no idea who you resonate with.

You don't know what nourishes you and what destroys you.
And yet… you want love?

You still confuse lust with love.
You chase the body, not the soul.
You see people through the lens of how much they turn you on
or how much validation they give you.

And then you feel empty.
Because how many times can you consume someone's body
while your soul is starving for truth?

You don't have humility. You just have opinions.
You know everything about relationships—
but nothing about yourself.
You think you're mature—
but can't even say "I'm sorry" without grinding your teeth.

Real love isn't for people who want to be right.
It's for those who've softened.

You don't have rituals.
Your days are random.
You expect love to save you, complete you, fill the void.
But nothing can fill someone
who's hollow on the inside.

You don't understand energy.
You don't believe in masculine and feminine poles.
But those are what dance in a relationship.
Masculine presence.
Feminine sensitivity.
Only together they create Home.

But you?
You still carry tension in your jaw and stiffness in your spine.
You're not present.

So how can you offer safety?
How can you receive trust?

You're still afraid of silence.

You always have to speak, text, explain, prove.
But true intimacy begins in the silence that isn't awkward—
it's sacred.

If you can't be quiet with someone without falling apart—
you're not ready for love.
Because a relationship is not just words.
It's energy.
It's breath.
It's presence.

You chase trends that say you should be "everything and nothing."
You erase polarity in the name of equality.
You accept disconnection in the name of acceptance.

But love needs polarity.
Tension.
Difference.
Sacredness.

You can't plant love in a wasteland.
But that's exactly where you're trying to grow it.

 So before you ask, "Why can't I have a deep relationship?"
Ask yourself:

Am I honest with myself?
Can I sit in silence?
Does my body feel safe?
Do I understand my own energy?
Do my words heal or destroy?
Does my sexuality serve my soul—or just my ego?
Can I look someone in the eyes—and say nothing?

Because love isn't a prize.
It's a process.
It's alchemy.
It's a fire that burns away your ego and leaves only what's real.

Not ready? That's okay.

But stop pretending you are.

Because real love won't come
until *you* become real.

Author's Note:
This isn't a soft hug in chapter form.
This is a mirror.
If it triggers you—it means you needed it.

🐍 DON'T TRY TO EARN IT. JUST BE.

Sometimes you look at a man standing in front of you and think,
"This can't be real.
There's too much light in him.
It hurts just to look at this kind of beauty."
And instead of walking away,
he steps closer.

And says that *you* are the one not from this world.

And then you want to hide.
Because... how can he not see your wounds?
Your fears, your breakdowns,
your nights when you clung to life with nothing but a clenched jaw?

But he sees.
And he doesn't run.
He doesn't want to fix you.
He doesn't try to earn you.

He just wants to be there.
He doesn't make himself a hero.
Doesn't try to outshine your past.
He simply... stays.
With a soul in his hand
and a body that doesn't want to conquer you
but just hold you – without conditions.

And that's when your mind starts to panic.
Because this was supposed to be harder.
He was supposed to overlook you.
He was supposed to leave.
He was supposed to crumble under your intensity.

But he doesn't.
And the more you show,
the more he wants to stay.

He says it's an honor to get to know you.
And you think,
"God, how is this possible?
Doesn't he know that knowing me means meeting my demons too?"

But that's exactly what he wants to learn.
Not to tame them.
But to know how to hold you when they rise again.

I don't know if anyone can ever truly be ready for this.
But I know one thing—
I don't need someone who tries to *earn* me.
I don't need a perfect man who always gets it right.
I need someone who doesn't run
when I'm no longer radiant.
Who stays
when I say again,
"I'm not sure I can do this."

Because love doesn't happen *because of* something.
It happens *despite* everything.

And when he looked at me and simply said,
"I'm here"—
I breathed like I do after a storm.
With relief.
With faith.
With that quiet thought:
"Maybe I'm not from this world.
But maybe he isn't either."

AUTHOR'S NOTE

This isn't about finding someone to carry you.
This is about someone who sits beside you when you collapse –
and simply says, "Scoot over."
No cape.
Just presence.
That's the real kind of magic.

🐾 I DON'T NEED TO FALL IN LOVE.

I just need to feel you.

A fter everything.
   After the emotional war,
   after the bloodstained battles for love,
after peeling yourself off illusions
and fighting your own shadow.
After nights in ruins and mornings in armor.

After all the "never again,"
"I'm done,"
"I'll never fall in love"—
suddenly,
someone appears.

He doesn't ride in on a white horse.
He doesn't throw his arms around you.
He doesn't promise to save you.

He just *is*.

Present.
Grounded.
He doesn't ask a hundred questions.
He doesn't try to figure you out.
He doesn't say he'll change you.
Or that you're too much—
too strong, too sensitive, too anything.

He just… feels you.

And for the first time in a long time,
you don't project.
You don't overanalyze.
You don't ask yourself if this *means* anything.

You're not dreaming of joint mortgages,
engagement rings,
or whether your lives will align.

You just *feel* the person.
The energy.
The depth.
The warmth.
The calm.

It doesn't have to be love.
It doesn't have to be some grand story out of a movie.
It can be something far more primal:
"I feel you."

Like in *Avatar*,
when one looks at the other and says,
"I see you."
But it's not about the eyes.
It's about the soul.

"I truly see you."
No armor.
No filters.
No pretending.

Because maybe the biggest gift on this road you've walked
isn't a fairytale love with a happy ending.
Maybe it's meeting someone
who doesn't want to fix a single thing in you.
Someone who doesn't pull you down.
Doesn't dim your light.
Just breathes beside you.
And sees you.
And feels you.

But to feel that—
you had to go through it all.

You had to break.
Fall apart.
Curse, cry, collapse.
Scream into your pillow.
Disappear.
Go silent.
Return to life with your soul scraped raw.

You had to walk through every damn chapter.
You had to stop believing in fairytales—
so you could finally believe in *yourself*.
You had to be reborn.

And only then—
could you attract someone
who felt your soul

because your soul was no longer searching for a savior.

It was searching for another soul.
One that wasn't afraid of depth.
One that wasn't afraid of *you*.

This isn't about butterflies.
It's not about the high of falling.
It's not about the prince.

It's about a human
who looks through your eyes—
and doesn't need to say a thing,
because you already know.

It's about that one moment
when, for the first time in your life,
you think:

I don't need to fall in love.
I just need to feel you.
And that's enough.

AUTHOR'S NOTE
Sometimes the deepest love isn't loud.
It's quiet recognition.
Two souls exhaling at the same time—
without needing to explain why.

A SOUL'S JOURNAL
RETURNING HOME

I didn't plan this book.
It simply happened.
Chapter by chapter — as my emotions unfolded.
I didn't write it from my head.
I wrote it from my body. From my heart. From my soul.

This isn't a love story.
This is a record of coming back to myself —
through meeting someone who saw me.
Fully.

Not perfectly. Not finished.

But real.
Full of fear, disbelief, strength, and softness — all at once.

Every sentence in this book was born from something that actually happened.
From a single text message.
From a pause between replies.
From one word he said.
From silence that healed.

This is not a book about falling in love.
This is a soul's journal — a return home.

But returning home isn't always gentle.
Sometimes it hurts.
Sometimes you have to walk through darkness just to trust the light again.
Sometimes you have to stand still — even when every part of you wants to run.

This book holds everything:
My hesitation.
My demons.
My fear of not being chosen again.
My sighs as I fell asleep with his words behind my eyelids.
My "I can't," tangled with "but maybe it's worth it."

It's a book about how love doesn't always come at the right time.
But when it comes — you recognize it instantly.
Because every cell in your body says: *This is it. This is now. This is him.*

This isn't a fairytale.
This is truth — written in emotion.
In thoughts. In touch. In hope.

So if you're looking for a sugar-coated fantasy — put this book back down.
But if something in you has been longing…
If some part of you still believes in a love that truly sees you —

then come in.

This isn't just our story.
It's yours too.
It's about the fact that *you* can find your way back home.

AUTHOR'S NOTE

You don't find home by searching for someone to save you.
You find it the moment you stop hiding who you are —
and someone still stays.

HE DIDN'T COME TO WIN ME OVER.

He Came to Heal Me.

He didn't make noise.
He didn't beat drums.
He didn't promise me the stars.

He simply walked into my life — quiet, attentive,
like he'd always known my world.
Like he understood, even before I said a word.

He didn't want to *have* me.

He wanted to *be*.
Beside me. With me.
Not for himself — but for *us*.

He didn't ask a hundred questions.
He didn't dig through my past.
He didn't tally up my scars.

Instead, he brought something I can't name.
Something you can't see — but you feel it in every cell of your body.
Something that doesn't say "stay,"
yet somehow makes you never want to leave.

He was like coming home to a place
you didn't even know existed.

He didn't touch my body to claim me —
he touched my soul to understand me.

He wasn't afraid of my darkness.
Or the storm I carry inside.
He didn't want to fix me.

He just stayed.

And his presence felt like a bandage, not a scalpel.

He didn't play the savior.
He didn't pose as a hero.
But he saved me anyway —
no fireworks, no grand gestures.

Just by being himself.

People like that don't *happen*.
They arrive.
Like a miracle.
Like breath after years of suffocating on life.

And I know one thing:
He will leave me better than he found me.

AUTHOR'S NOTE

Sometimes the people who heal you
don't even know they're doing it.
They're just being real.
And that's what saves you.

DUM SPIRO SPERO – AS LONG AS YOU BREATHE

I thought it was over.
Not life — life keeps going.
Bills need paying. Kids need raising. The car needs gas.
But love...?
Love was dead.
Buried in a coffin that read: *"Too late."*

I closed the lid and covered it in silence.

I didn't believe anymore.
Not in fairy tales. Not in sparks. Not in "meant to be."
I was done with heartbreaks, longing, pretending that "maybe this means something."
I was done loving for two.

I had learned to live alone.
Strong. Independent. Sharp.

I rebuilt myself from pieces —
after a childhood without a mother,
after an emotional executioner for a partner,
after every night I sat alone asking myself,
"Is this all there is?"

And then...
No, no prince came.
There were no fanfares.
He didn't write, *"You're the one."*
He didn't say he'd save me from loneliness.

He just... was.
With tenderness in his eyes.
With maturity in his words.
With space — for *me*.

Not to heal me.
Just to **be**.

And suddenly, what seemed impossible... became possible.
Not because I was looking.
Not because I was ready.
But because I was still breathing.

Dum Spiro Spero.
As long as you breathe — you can still meet someone.
As long as you breathe — not everything is lost.
As long as you breathe — life can still write a new script.

Not a fairytale.

But truth.

You don't need to be twenty,
or have the perfect body,
or a clean story,
or a heart without scars.

You can be fifty-two,
with six kids,
a chaotic past,
and still...
feel tenderness so real, it hurts.

Because love doesn't come to the perfect.
It comes to those who've stopped searching —
but still need it.

So if you think it's too late — don't believe it.
If you feel too broken — don't believe it.
If you're afraid no one will ever look at you with wonder — don't
believe it.

As long as you breathe — you can start again.

Now look at me.

A woman who's been through emotional hell.
Who carries stories too heavy for coffee table talk.
Who spent years trying to *deserve* love instead of simply being
loved.
Who raised six children, had her heart broken,
and a thousand reasons never to trust again.

And still...
I breathe.
I feel.
I love.

And I know:
If I could feel my heart beating again —
so can you.

Not everything is lost.
Not everything is behind you.
You'll be surprised how much beauty still waits for you.
You'll fall in love again.
With someone.
With life.
With yourself.

Dum Spiro Spero.
As long as you breathe — everything is possible.

AUTHOR'S NOTE

Hope doesn't live in fairy tales.
It lives in the quiet pulse beneath your ribs.
If you're still breathing — you're still becoming.

❧ ENCOUNTERS WRITTEN IN THE STARS

Some encounters are so unreal,
you don't even know if they truly happened — or if you just dreamed them.
Or maybe... they were written somewhere higher.
In the stars.
In the blueprint of your soul.
Someone appears.
Just like that.

No fanfare. No warning.

A stranger — but somehow, not.
Like you've known him forever.
Like you recognize his soul in a split second.

He looks at you the way no one ever has.
And you feel it —
you're no longer alone.
Someone actually *sees* you.

Not just your hair, your eyes, your words.
But *you*.

The mess inside.
The wounds, the scars.
The hunger to be loved,
the fear of messing it all up — again.

And even though you don't say a word —
he knows.

This isn't a fairytale.
This isn't "happily ever after."
It's not flowers and candlelit dinners.
It's something so much bigger.

It's a remembering.
Of who you truly are.
Of who you were before you started pretending.
Before life broke you.
Before you learned it's safer not to feel.

Before you became fluent in
"I'm fine,"
"I've got this."

Because it's this kind of love — not sweet, not sparkly —
but raw, naked, real —
that rips your soul apart.

So you can finally rebuild it

the way *you* want.
Not the way they told you to.

And it all starts so simply.
A message.
A meeting.
A voice on the phone.
A glance.

And suddenly you *know* —
nothing will be the same.

It's not a coincidence.
The Universe just shoved you
into heaven or hell.
Or maybe both at once.

He reaches out before you even have time to miss him.
He enters your space like he already knows the way.
Like he's always had the key.

And it doesn't matter how old you are.
Where you're from.
Who you were before.

He's here for a reason.

This meeting wakes you up.
Freezes time.
Shatters your carefully arranged life.
Breaks every pattern.
Drags every demon out of the basement.

And it hurts.
God, it hurts.

But you can't stop.

Because it's not just falling in love.
It's something else.
A threshold.

They call it many things —

a soulmate. A mirror.

Doesn't matter.

Because deep down,
you know one thing:

No one has ever moved you this deeply.
No one has ever touched the buried parts of you
so gently…
and so violently
at the same time.

And even if you run.
Even if you're scared.
Even if you tell yourself this can't be real —
he stays in you.

And maybe that's why he came.
Not to stay forever.

But to open something inside you.
To show you it was always there.

He didn't *create* it.
He just laid a finger on the wounds
that never fully healed.

And they finally started bleeding.

It's not a punishment.
It's a chance.
For truth.

For being yourself — without the mask.
For being *seen* — without performing "put-together," "polite,"
"strong."

But only
if you have the courage to look someone in the eye.
Not him —
you.

He was the mirror.

Now it's your turn.

AUTHOR'S NOTE

Some people don't come to love you.
They come to wake you.
And once your soul opens,
you'll never fit back into the life you had before.

🐒 "HE ORDERED
ME IN JANUARY.
AND I CAME."

(a story about how the universe doesn't hear your words — but your intention)

This wasn't a drawing made by hand.
There was no pencil.
No artist's intuition.
No knowledge of my face.
Just a few typed words.
A few qualities.
A few intentions.
And a need.

Not the kind that screams —
but the kind that travels through the universe
faster than sound.

In January,
he typed a prompt into an AI image generator.
A description of the kind of woman he'd like to meet. To love.
Not to create her.
Just... to see if she could exist.

A strong woman.
And soft at the same time.
Warm. Gentle.
With wise eyes.
With a story carved into her soul,
and a light that hadn't gone out — despite everything.

When he showed it to me...
I froze.

It was me.
Not *kind of like me*.
Not *close in energy*.
It was *me*.

My face.
My expression.
My shape.

My presence.

I had never been photographed in that pose —
but the moment I saw it, I knew.
That was me.

He didn't know me then.
Didn't have my photo.
Didn't know what I looked like.

But the Universe knew.
And it answered.

Not that day.
Not that week.
But when everything aligned.
When we were both ready —
we met.

Not by chance.
Not "just one of those things."
It was too precise.
Too strong.
Too familiar.

So I started wondering…
Is it really possible?

Can you actually *call* someone in?
Not like ordering a package.
But like inviting a presence.
A readiness.
A soul that whispers, *"I'm here — if you are too."*

Because maybe that's how the Universe works.
Maybe it doesn't grant wishes —
it answers vibration.
It responds to the quality of your intention.
To your willingness to meet truth.

Maybe it really does read between the lines.

It wasn't just a graphic.
It was a calling.
No words.
No delivery date.
No guarantee.

And maybe that's why I came.

Because it wasn't desperate seeking.
It was an invitation.
And I heard it.

And now I think about it often.
How sometimes,
we're already part of someone's life
long before we ever meet them.

We're drawn —
in hearts,
in dreams,
in intentions,
in the quiet question:
"Could someone like that even exist?"

And when you're in alignment with yourself —
things start to line up.

Not because you've earned it.
But because you're ready.

So don't laugh when someone tells you they "ordered" you.
Because maybe they did.
Not through a form.
Not through a prayer.
But through the courage to *feel* —
and not pretend they don't.

And you?
You can call in something real too.
Not with a checklist.
But by being yourself.

All the way down to the bone.

Because the Universe doesn't give you what you want.
It gives you what you're ready to *become*.

AUTHOR'S NOTE

Your truth is the most powerful signal you'll ever send.
Say it with your energy — not your words.
The right person will hear it. Even if you whisper.

SYNCHRONIZATION — WHEN LIFE STARTS SPEAKING YOUR LANGUAGE

A t first, everything feels like coincidence.
You think it's fate.
A random message.
A chance encounter.
A book that falls off the shelf at the exact moment it needs to.
A line overheard on the radio.
A man who suddenly says something you've been thinking for
months —
but couldn't find the words for.
But then you start to realize — they're not accidents.
They're answers.

They arrive when you finally start asking questions
from the level of your soul.
Not from fear.
Not from control.
Not from need.
But from truth.

That's what synchronization is.
It's like typing your inner self into the Universe's Google —
and it sends you exactly what your soul needs.

But only when you're ready.
When you stop pretending.
When you stop forcing.
When you start being yourself —
painfully, entirely, honestly.

And suddenly, everything begins to align.

It's like walking into a store full of chaos
and your eyes land on one dress. Just one.
The one that feels like someone stitched it
from your memories, your fears, your longings, your colors.

And when you put it on — you don't doubt it for a second.

It's not just a dress.
It's your second skin.

That's how synchronization works.
You attract people, conversations, decisions, moments
that fit you so precisely
it's like they were sewn by the Hand of the Divine Seamstress.

To your soul.
To your energy.
To your maturity.
To the exact place you are now.

Not before.
Not later.
Now.

Because only now are you ready.
Only now do you know who you are.
What you're no longer willing to accept.
And what you truly long for.

And then,
everything starts speaking your language.

You don't have to push.
You don't have to chase signs.
You don't have to prove anything to the world.

Because the world starts syncing with *you*.

Because synchronization doesn't come from chaos.
It comes from truth.

And truth…
is the purest form of love.

AUTHOR'S NOTE

The moment you stop chasing what's not for you,
everything meant for you knows exactly where to find you.
All it needed was your honesty.

🐾 I DON'T KNOW IF I CAN.

But I Know I Have to Try.

T his isn't regular fear.
It's not, "I'm afraid he'll hurt me."
It's deeper.
It's that moment when you look into someone's eyes and think,

"Fuck. If I don't screw this up, this could be something real."
And that's exactly when the fear gets worse.

Because you're not scared of *him*.
You're scared of *you*.

What if I can't handle this?
What if I — with my wrecked insides,
with all this baggage —
am the biggest threat to something good?

What if I fall back into what I know best —
the storm,
the chase,
the high of wanting someone who doesn't want to be caught?

Because with him... it's different.
There are no games.
No masks.
No tug-of-war.

He's just... there.
Present.
Interested.
Gentle.

And that scares the shit out of me.
Because I don't know what to do with the quiet.
With the calm.
With the safety.

Because my whole life,
I've been trained to survive.
Not to love.
Not to be close.
To *survive*.

I've always fought for attention.
For approval.
For someone to finally see that I was worth loving.

And now?

Now someone just sees me.
And doesn't run.

And that's exactly why I wanted to run.

Because there was no heart-punch.
No butterflies.
No panic over whether he'd text back.

There was… peace.
And for me, that's foreign.
Almost disturbing.

I started to wonder — is this it?
Have I stopped feeling?
Is this peace or emotional numbness?

Maybe my body has learned survival so well
it shuts down anything that isn't chaos.

I felt like someone gave me a handful of tranquilizers.
Or like I was a little bit high.
Not hurting —
but not buzzing either.

No high.
No crash.
No euphoria.
Just… good.

And that?
That's a new kind of drug for me.

And I don't know if I'm ready to get addicted.

Because I'm that emotional junkie.
I need drama to feel alive.
I need screaming to know I exist.

And now?
Now there's only silence.
And a touch that doesn't want to claim me —
just hold me.

And it's driving me insane.

And still...
I don't want to destroy this.

Because maybe this *is* it.
Maybe this is the new chapter.
The one where you learn to love
not through pain —
but through presence.

Maybe this is the kind of relationship
that doesn't scream *"LOVE ME"*
but whispers,
"Stay. You don't have to be afraid anymore."

Maybe this is the kind of man you're not afraid of —
because you know he won't run.

Because he's got his demons too.
And he's scared too.

And maybe that's exactly why it could work.
Because we both know what it means to fall apart.
And we both want to build something.

Not out of fireworks.
Not out of impulse.
But out of breath.
Out of stillness.
Out of choice.

I don't know if I can.
But I know this —
if I don't try,
I'll never forgive myself.

AUTHOR'S NOTE

Not every beginning has to explode.

Sometimes love walks in quietly —
and dares you to stay.

🐾 THE AWAKENING OF LOVE

N ot every woman is ready to truly love.
And not every man is ready to be truly seen.
But when She finally becomes herself—truly herself—
when she no longer plays, pretends, waits, or fights—
when she starts living from the inside out...
She no longer needs anyone to "complete" her.

And it's exactly then—

that He appears.

Not because she was searching.
Not because she was "ready."
But because their souls… had known each other before.

This doesn't happen by accident.
It's the kind of encounter that defies logic.
As if two people heard the same sound inside.
A song they knew before they ever learned to speak.

And when She looks at Him…
she knows this isn't a new story.
It's a return.
To a place they've been before.
To each other.

Because an Awakened Woman draws in an Awakened Man.
Not one who needs her light to chase away his shadows.
But one who has already walked through his darkness.
And returned from it—truer, deeper, quiet in a different way.

He doesn't want to fight her fire.
He sees her.
He isn't scared of her intensity.
He doesn't try to tame it.
Because he knows flame.

And when they meet…
there are no games. No masks. No "should I?"

There is vulnerability.
There is raw truth.
There are hands reaching without fear.

This isn't a romance.
It's a calling.
It's a descent into depth.
It's love that isn't afraid of shadow, hunger, or soul.

She won't pretend she doesn't feel.
And he won't run from what he feels.

She won't settle for a man who only shows what's easy.
Because she knows—
if his heart isn't open,
everything else is just a performance.

He won't seek a woman he can have.
He'll seek the one he can *be with*.

And when they find each other…
love becomes a prayer.
Touch becomes sacred.
Words grow quiet—because there's nothing left to prove.

It's not easy.
But it's real.

And maybe that's why…
it's so rare.

Author's Note:
This is not a fairytale about a prince on a white horse.
And it's not a manual for attracting "the right kind of man."
This is a story about what happens when you stop searching…
and start living in your truth—
Because everything real, especially love,
finds you there.
Even Him.

🐍TWIN FLAMES DON'T SEARCH.

They Recognize.

It wasn't magic.
No fireworks.
No angels singing in the background.
No signs from the heavens.

Just one look.
And silence.

A silence where you didn't have to say a word —
and I already knew.

I knew this wasn't the first time.

That somewhere, somewhen —
we'd already met.

That your eyes were telling a story
my soul still remembered.

Because twin flames don't start from the beginning.
They *remember*.

What Are Twin Flames, Really?

It's not a fairytale.
Not a poetic slogan.

It's the real meeting of two souls
who came here for something more.

A twin flame doesn't fall in love with your face,
your charm,
your achievements.

They fall for *you* —
the real you,
under all the layers.

They're the one holding your soul
when your hands have already let go.

The one who never makes you prove your worth.

Who knows your silence isn't emptiness —
it's everything in you trembling at once.

How Do They Know?

By the look.
By the silence.

By that strange feeling in your stomach —
not butterflies.
Home.

By the way everything flows,

without force,
without rush.

By the way you can cry without explanation
and he doesn't ask,
"What's wrong?"
He just says,
"I'm here."

By the way you're not afraid to be naked —
not your body.
Your soul.

By the way he knows you
better than you've ever known yourself.

Why Do They Meet?

Not for the easy ride.
Not to build a perfect Instagram life.
Not to kiss under cherry trees
and live happily ever after.

They meet to *grow*.
To face lessons.
To finish something.
To repair what was once broken.

A twin flame can blow your life to pieces.
And then help shape you into someone
truer,
stronger,
calmer.

It's not a convenient love.
It's a *transformational* one.

And Still... I Know It's You.

Because with you,
I don't have to be perfect.

I can be bruised.
Tired.
Silent —
and you still *hear* me.

I feel you before you even walk in.
I miss you even when you're sitting next to me.

Because a twin flame isn't just presence —
it's connection.

And even if life pulls us apart for a while,
even if we lose each other along the way —

I already know.

You are my home.
And I…
I am your way back to yourself.

AUTHOR'S NOTE

Some people don't arrive.
They *return*.
And you feel it in your bones.

❧ LET LOVE BE THE ONE THING THAT'S SIMPLE

L ove shouldn't feel like a race.
It shouldn't be constant tension,
that sick fear you'll mess up again —
say one word too much
or one sentence too little.
That you'll be "too much."
Or not enough.

Always *wrong* somehow.

Love isn't a minefield you tiptoe across.
Love is peace.
That deep, silent *exhale* you feel
when you're with him
and suddenly... nothing hurts.

It doesn't mean there won't be hard talks.
It doesn't mean you'll never fight
or that everything will play out
like a romantic comedy.

No.
But even in the middle of a storm,
you should feel the *us*.
That you're holding each other through it.
That you don't have to fight
just to breathe.

Love is supposed to lift you.
Not break your wings.
It should raise you,
not crush you with quiet expectations
and unspoken demands.

You should feel *seen*.
Wanted.
Worthy of everything —
even when you're in your old sweats,
with a red nose and your hair tied up
with a scrunchie from another lifetime.

Love isn't just made of picture-perfect moments.
Not just the ones hashtagged
#blessed.

It's also:
– the kiss good morning,
– coffee brought to bed,

– shared silence that asks for nothing,
– arguing in the grocery store over what's for dinner,
– caring when your throat hurts,
– a hand on your back in a crowd —
just so you know you're his.

That, too, is love.
And it's in these ordinary, quiet things
where the truth shows up.

Because love is a choice.
A daily one.
Sometimes easy.
Sometimes hard.
But always intentional.

It's not *just* passion.
Sure, passion matters —
without it, things wither.

But passion alone
won't carry the weight.
Sex won't replace presence.
An orgasm won't heal
the kind of loneliness you feel
inside a relationship.

Love is being someone's *safe place*.
Their *relief*.
The one who soothes,
who eases the ache,
who doesn't add more fire
to the hell they're already carrying.

It doesn't have to be grand.
It doesn't have to be cinematic.
It doesn't have to be perfect.

It just has to be real.

Because in a world

that keeps spinning off the rails —
let love be the one thing
that's still simple.

AUTHOR'S NOTE

And if it ever feels too hard —
maybe it's not love.
Maybe it's a lesson,
wearing love's clothes.

🐾 TAKE OFF THE ARMOR, LAY DOWN THE SWORD.

Love That Doesn't Hurt.

I didn't know it existed.
I didn't know you could fall in love… quietly.
Without euphoria.

Without butterflies.
Without that insane rollercoaster of:
He loves me. He vanishes.
I didn't know there could be a man
with whom you don't have to perform.
Don't have to fight.
Don't have to prove a damn thing.
You just are.
And that's enough.

Every past relationship taught me one thing:
Always be ready for an attack.
Always keep your sword in hand,
armor strapped to your heart,
and an escape plan tucked in your back pocket—
just in case he turns out to be
another coward in a prince's costume.

And then someone shows up...
and somehow, you just *know.*
With your whole body.
With every cell.
With every scar.

You know you're safe.

It's not a movie feeling.
It's not words crafted to seduce you.
It's not another promise made of air.
It's something you *feel.*

The silence between messages doesn't make you anxious.
The unanswered text doesn't awaken your fear.
There's no need to "control,"
to "decode,"
to "read between the lines."

There's no internal panic:
"Why hasn't he replied?"
"Did I mess up?"

"Does he still want me?"

Because you *know.*
You know you can lean in.
You can fall.
You can shut your eyes and fly —
and no one's going to let you hit the ground.

And you know what?
This is just the beginning.
You don't yet know where it's going.
You can't call it some great love story — not yet.
But you know it's *something more.*

It's a *knowing.*
Of *someone.*
With every fiber of your being.

Because for the first time — you're calm.
Because every part of you feels
you're not alone this time.
That this time… it might just work.

That you've got your own bodyguard now.
Of your heart.
And your soul.

No fireworks.
No drama.
No fucking games.

There's conversation.
Laughter.
A quiet, *"Thank you for being here."*

There's a decision —
not to keep searching.
That this is enough.
And it all unfolds so naturally.

No grand entrances.
Just a peace so steady,

you finally want to hang up your armor
and shove it deep in the closet.
You won't be needing it anymore.

Because *this*
is the kind of love that doesn't need saving.
Doesn't need decoding.
Doesn't need to be feared.

This is love that doesn't hurt.
And you never knew it was real.
But it is.

And even if it ends in a week,
a month,
a year — or ten —
you'll know it was worth it.

Worth knowing this kind of love.
This kind of peace.
This kind of certainty —
that you're done looking back.
And you're always,
always one step forward now.

ATHOR'S NOTE

Maybe the greatest plot twist in your life
is that love turns out to be
quiet.
And real.
And safe.
And that you were never broken —
just armed for the wrong kind of war.

I CAN'T PROMISE THIS WILL WORK OUT

But I promise I'll be honest with you.
(from *The Woman You Can't Forget*)

We've known each other for four days.
Four days—and it feels like four lifetimes.
Ripped out of time, removed from logic.

Not yet defined by reason, but already written into my body.
I wasn't planning anything.
Not to get close.
Not to kiss you.
Because things like that—you don't plan.
They just happen.
And when they do—everything else goes silent.
Even fear.

But still… I feel it.
Not fear of *you.*
Fear of what this is doing to me.
Of how deeply I feel it.
Of what it means to feel safe again—only to maybe fall again, even harder.

I was always scared to say how I felt.
In every past relationship.
Because whenever I spoke, they vanished.
They froze.
They pulled away.
And it hurt.

But now I know I have to speak.
With every cell of my body, I know I have to be honest.
Even if the truth stings a little.
I have to be real.
For you.
For me.
For us—if there's ever going to be an "us."

Because I can't promise this will work out.
I don't know what this is yet.
I won't paint a perfect picture.
But I'll promise you one thing: I'll be real.
I'll say what I feel.
I won't go quiet.
I won't disappear into fear.

Just… give me a moment.
Give me space to breathe into this.

Because today, when you kissed my forehead,
it meant more than a thousand kisses on the mouth.
It said, *"You matter. I'm here. I want to protect you."*

And that… broke through everything.
Through every layer of armor, through all the cautiousness,
through every survival reflex.

Because *that* is how I want to be loved.
Without a plan.
Without a script.
Without masks.
Just a forehead kissed by someone's heart.

Author's Note:
If you're looking for fairy tales, keep scrolling.
This is the kind of love that makes you flinch before you fall.
And still—you fall.

🦢 PEACE. THE KIND THAT MAKES YOU WANT TO CRY.

Y ou know what I was most afraid of?
That it was going to be bullshit. Again.
That I'd get swept up in emotions, only to be left staring at an empty phone and a silence that hurts more than any scream.
Yesterday I was shaking.
Pissed off.
Terrified that once again, I was walking into something blind.
That once again, it was too good to be true.
Just a phase, just words, just infatuation —

And soon I'd be stuck asking, *"What did I do wrong?"*

But today…
Today is quiet.
Not the suffocating kind, when you're waiting for a text.
But the good kind. Soft. Safe.
The kind of quiet that makes you feel *certain.*

I don't have to guess.
Don't have to analyze.
Don't have to climb into his head.

Because he talks.
He shows up.
He's simply **there**.

No games.
No disappearing acts.
No *"sorry, I was busy"* as the default excuse for emotional absence.

He didn't vanish.
I didn't have to send ten messages to get one *"hey."*
I didn't have to remind him I exist, play hard to get, or pretend I didn't care just to spark interest.

No.
He was just… there.
He woke up after a night shift and the first thing he did was text:
"Good morning, my happiness."

Then he called. Just like that.
Didn't wait for *"Can you talk?"*
Didn't overthink if it was "appropriate."
He wanted to hear my voice.
Told me what he felt all night.
How he missed me.
How he told his coworker he'd met the woman of his life.

And you know what?
I don't know what will happen in a month.

I don't know what we'll be in a year.
But **I know what's happening now.**

And right now...
There's a man saying:
*"I'll skip my Sunday shift, even if it's the biggest contract of the year.
I'll make it up on Monday. But I want to be with you on Sunday."*

Not *"if I get a chance."*
Not *"if it fits in my schedule."*
With you. On Sunday. Because you matter most.

This isn't some Hollywood love confession.
It's not rings and rose petals and vows made during a honeymoon high.
It's the **daily loyalty**.
The quiet, grounded, real kind.

It's the way I feel *wanted.*
Not as a distraction.
Not as an escape.
Not as some emotional fast-food.

But as **someone who matters.**
Someone worth changing plans for.
Someone who doesn't have to beg for time.
Someone who doesn't fight to be a "priority" — she just *is.*

And then comes that moment...
when you sit with a cup of coffee and think,
"Damn. This is it. This is what peace feels like."

You're not afraid of silence anymore.
You don't measure love in emojis.
You don't feel stupid for texting first.

You feel... **held.**
Not because he *gives* you anything.
But because around him, you don't have to pretend anymore.

Author's Note:

This chapter doesn't end with *"happily ever after."*
It doesn't need to.
It ends with peace.
And the quiet knowing that someone finally chose *you* —
no conditions, no manipulation, no games.
And maybe, just maybe...
you finally chose yourself too.

🐦 AN ORDINARY MORNING

I don't even know how to describe this feeling.
Because really—it's nothing special.
Just an ordinary morning.
Just a cup of coffee in bed.
Just your arm still smelling like sleep and the touch of the night before.
Just that soft "just a little longer," whispered with your eyes still closed.
And yet...

It's more than the whole week.
More than all the texts, the photos, the longing, the waiting.

This one morning.
Right after the night when our bodies spoke the words we couldn't say.
Right before the day that rips us apart again.

We step out into the garden.
I'm wearing your hoodie. You're holding your tea.
We sit on the same bench where we've already promised each other—again and again—that we'll make it.
That we'll survive this one more week.

And I know goodbye is coming.
That slow, thirty-minute goodbye with a thousand hugs,
a thousand "I love you,"
a thousand "I miss you already,"
a thousand "please be safe."

It's the moment I fall apart—quietly.
I don't cry out loud anymore.
I break on the inside.
Silently.

This morning is everything.
It's our whole world, caught between one night and all the bullshit that waits for us after.
It's the last touch.
The last kiss.
The last look through the car window.

And then… silence.
Emptiness filled only with one sentence:
"Let's do whatever it takes to see each other again."

Author's Note:
I don't need breakfast in bed or trips to IKEA.
I need those ten minutes with my head on your shoulder.

Because that's where my home lives.

🐿 WHEN SOULS RECOGNIZE EACH OTHER

This isn't something you learn.

This isn't the kind of relationship you build step by step.

It's not a connection that grows from logic, from dating books, from checklists, or a strategy to find *"the ideal partner."*

It's resonance.

It's a meeting that didn't really happen now.

It's two souls who already knew each other—

only the body hasn't remembered yet.

It's a feeling you can't quite name.
You're not falling in love.
You just know him.
Not from life.
Not from memories.
Not from anything you can explain.
But from a deep, metaphysical place inside you that opens without resistance—
at the sound of his voice,
the scent of his skin,
the vibration of his presence.

Because you don't choose this connection.
The connection chooses you.

When souls recognize each other,
everything goes quiet.
And clear.

You don't have to do anything.
You don't have to earn it.
You don't have to try.
He sees you as you are.

Not how you look.
Not how you speak.
Not how you perform your role.
But how you *vibrate*.

How you light up when you're simply yourself.

This isn't flirting.
It's not chemistry.
It's an exchange of soul codes.
Like a lantern inside you lights up—
and somehow, without knowing how,
he knows the way to it in the dark.

It happens beyond time.

Beyond logic.
Beyond control.

It lives in the energetic field between your bodies,
in micro-movements,
in an intuition that whispers:
"Don't be afraid. You're home."

It has nothing in common with dating.
You're not wondering if he likes you.
You're not counting the hours until he texts back.

Because his presence pierces through every layer of fear.
He doesn't need to be loud.
He just needs to exist.
And you already feel him.

You feel his soul.
And hers—she remembers you.

Not every woman will experience this.
Not every soul came to this world for it.
Not every heart is ready to hold something so powerful.

Because this connection dismantles you.
It leaves no space for games, illusions, or masks.
It doesn't let you retreat.

Because once you've felt this…
you know.

And even if you run, push away, or hide—
your whole field vibrates differently.
Because now you know what it's like to be seen without words.
To be read without touch.
To be felt—without fear.

This isn't a fairy tale.
It's not Keanu Reeves and background music.
It's quantum physics of the soul.

It's frequency.

It's the exchange of vibrations.
It's a world they never taught you about.
But once you've tasted it—
you never forget.

You might forget the sound of his voice.
You might forget the lines of his face.
But you'll never forget what your soul felt when it met his.

And when you ask yourself, *"How do I know him?"*
The answer won't come from your mouth.
It'll rise from your heart.

You know him—
because your soul knows the way to his.
And that's not something you learn.
It's something you... **feel.**

Author's Note:
Listen... I honestly don't know how to explain it to you.
It's not some story you tell over wine and gossip.
It's not *"who made the first move"* or *"does he find me attractive?"*
Hell, it's not even a story *about a man.*

It's about energy.
About a soul recognizing another soul.
Looking across a room and saying without words:
"You're back. I waited. You're here now."

And then... everything inside me went silent.
No need to analyze.
No need to ask if it's safe or smart or makes any sense.

I just... *knew.*

It doesn't happen in the mind.
It happens in the body.
In the heart.
In something way beyond logic.

And yes, I know—

It might sound like a fairytale.
But it's not.

It's real.

🐾 A TOUCH THAT REMEMBERS THE SOUL

I don't know how to name it.
It's not love.
It's not desire.
It's... something else.
Something that lives in the silence between words.
Something that grows where the light can't reach.
I miss him.

But not the way you miss someone's body.
I miss his presence.
His calm.
That part of me that doesn't have to play any role when he's near.

Like we knew each other… before time.

And even when I look at his photo—
nothing stirs inside me.
No shiver.
No warmth under the skin.

And yet… I miss him when he's silent.
I miss his voice when he doesn't write.
I miss the space I could just *be* in—without proving anything.

It's always been the opposite.
First touch.
First desire.
First impulse.
Then maybe a conversation.
Maybe feelings.
Maybe more.
But the body always came first—
like it was trying to make up for what the soul lacked.

And here?

The body is quiet.
It doesn't resist.
But it doesn't ache either.
It waits.
As if it doesn't want to interrupt the soft melody that's starting
to form.

He doesn't rush either.
He doesn't pull.
He doesn't test my limits.
As if he knows: the most sacred things aren't grabbed—
they're held.

With care.
With reverence.
With silence in the heart.

He touched my hand like he was holding something priceless.
Not like a woman.
Not like skin.
But like memory.
Like something he's known forever, only forgot for a while.

And when he kissed me…
It wasn't a kiss of hunger.
It was a kiss that asked:
"Are you really here?"
"Is it even possible that I found you?"

And then he pulled me close.
Not forcefully.
Just enough—
like he needed to make sure I was real.
Like he was holding the answer he'd been searching for his whole life.

I don't know if my body will ever fully open.
Maybe it will.
Maybe it won't.
But if it does—
I want it to be real.
Not from need.
Not from fear.
Not from loneliness.

Only from that place inside me that will say:
"Yes. Now I'm ready."

Because maybe, for the first time in my life—
I don't have to rush toward the body to save my soul.

Maybe for the first time—
it's the soul gently leading me toward the body.

Author's Note:
Let's just say…
He didn't grab my ass like the rest of them.
He touched my hand like he was touching a memory.
And maybe that's how you know—
when it's real.

🐾 SHE DOESN'T NEED A LEASH

Not every woman wants to keep a man on a short leash. Not every woman needs control, tracking apps, bans on guys' nights, or weekly message inspections.

A woman of worth doesn't crave power over him.

She already knows that real intimacy is not born from obedience.

She longs for peace.

The kind of peace you feel beside someone who knows his value

and stays loyal—
not because he *has* to,
but because he *chooses* to.

She respects a man with discipline.
Not one who says what you want to hear,
but one who speaks the truth.
Not someone who needs praise or handholding,
but someone who holds his own.

She no longer wants to change anyone.
She doesn't want to raise him.
She doesn't want to save him from his own chaos.

She's been the one who healed, who waited, who carried the weight for too long.
She's been stronger than her own fears.
She's tired of holding relationships together with bloody hands and broken hope.

Now she knows: **love is not therapy**.
It's not a rescue mission.
It's not about turning a boy into a man.

A mature woman craves presence—not drama.
Truth—not games.
Safety—not adrenaline.

She wants to trust—without control.
To love—without fear.
To stay close—without fighting for the basics.

Because real love doesn't need surveillance.
It needs **maturity, freedom, and mutual respect**.

This is not a story of two halves completing each other.
It's two whole worlds choosing to meet.

Not because they *need* to—
but because they *want* to.

Not because they *lack* something—

but because they *see* each other clearly, and still say: yes.

Author's Note:

You're not here to fix, save, or heal anyone. That's not your role. If he needs a leash to stay—maybe he's not the kind worth feeding.

🐍 THE DEMONS ALWAYS KNOCK LOUDER AT NIGHT

Sometimes I look at him and think—
This can't be real.
It's too soft. Too present. Too safe.
And I freeze.

Because my demons don't sleep.
They wait.

They wait for a moment like this—
when I finally start to believe that maybe, just maybe,
I deserve love.
And then they whisper:

"He's just pretending."
"It's only sex."
"He'll get what he wants and disappear."
"Any minute now he'll take off the mask—and you'll be left picking up your pieces. Again."

Because that's how it always ended, right?

I gave too much.
I felt too deeply.
I believed too quickly.
And then—boom. Silence. Withdrawal. Ghosting. Gaslighting.
Pain with no closure.

So now, even when everything is good—
my mind still flips the switch.

What if he's playing a role?
What if this tenderness is just strategy?
What if the way he holds me isn't love, just manipulation in disguise?

And yet... he's still here.
Every week.
Every touch.
Every word.
Nothing *he* does gives me a reason to doubt him.
Only my *past* does.

These demons—
they're mine.
Not his.

It's my trauma that screams louder than logic.

It's my body that remembers hands that hurt.
It's my nervous system that shakes even when his voice is calm and his presence is steady.

So sometimes I pull away.
Sometimes I go quiet.
Sometimes I hide in my shell because I *need* a moment.
To tell myself:
This is now. That was then.
He's not them. And I'm not that girl anymore.

Because I've done the work.
I've paid the price.
I've walked through every circle of hell with bare feet and a bleeding soul.

I'm not asking for a fairy tale.
But I'm done believing that love always has to hurt.

This time... I want it different.
This time... I want it soft.
And even if I shake, even if I flinch, even if I doubt—
I'll still choose to stay.
To trust.
To believe.

Because maybe this *is* my time.
Maybe I'm finally free.

Author's Note:
If he's faking it, he deserves an Oscar.
But if he's not...
then maybe this is what love actually looks like when it's real.

🐾 YOU'RE NOT BROKEN. IT'S PTSD

It's not because of ghosting.
Not because of a missed text.
Not because of a man who "changed his mind."
It's not because of fairy tales about emotionally unavailable men.
Not because your friends kept saying you attract the toxic ones.

It's because your body lived in a war zone for years.
It's because you spent a lifetime next to someone who never saw

you.
Someone who was always around—but never really with you.
Who had time for his games, his moods, his comfort—but never had time to ask if your kids had something to eat.

It's because of the relationships where you carried the weight of life alone.
Because of all the mornings you woke up asking:
"Will I have to do this by myself again today?"

It's because of abuse.
Real, brutal abuse—not the kind from memes.
Because of the yelling that stabbed into your brain like a knife.
Because of the hand that moved too fast.
Because of the eyes that looked at you like you were the enemy.

It's because of betrayal that came when you thought this time was real.
Because you were planning your wedding while he was fucking someone else in your bed.
Because you kept explaining to your children why Mommy is sad again.
Until at some point… there was only an echo left. The echo of who you used to be.

This isn't trauma from falling in love.
This is trauma from drowning and no one coming to save you.
From no one even asking if you were still alive.

You're not broken.
Your nervous system just learned that love = danger.
That touch = pain.
That closeness = a trap.
That anything good = a ticking bomb.
That tenderness = bait.

You're not hysterical.
Your body reacts like a soldier after war.
Your heart can't relax because too many times, someone cut it open the moment you let your guard down.

It's not "overreacting." It's PTSD.

You're not broken.
You're not crazy.
You're not "too sensitive."

What's happening to you... isn't drama. It's not "difficult personality."
It's PTSD.
Yes, that.
Post-Traumatic Stress Disorder.
Not just for soldiers.
Not just for survivors of war or disasters.
For women—like us.
After silent wars fought behind closed doors.

Sometimes all it takes is one louder word.
One fast glance.
One overly concerned tone.
A hand that moves too quickly.
A voice that sounds a little too much like *his*.
And that's it.
Everything lights up.
Fight or flight.
Tight jaw. Tense body.
Heart racing. Breath shallow.
ALERT. ALERT.
It's not him—it's the past.

Sometimes it's his kindness that scares me.
That he worries.
That he asks if I'm okay.
That he wants to hold me.

Because that's when my mind whispers: it's a trap.
That's how it started last time.
He was gentle first.
He said he loved me.
And then...

Then everything hurt.

So now... even kindness can trigger fear.

It's not logical.
It's not rational.
It's the body.
The body remembers.
The neurons remember.
The pain is still there.

This doesn't happen *because* I want it to.
It happens *despite* me.

Because I've been in relationships that weren't just toxic.
They were destructive.
A relationship with a narcissist—daily manipulation, gaslighting, being told I'm the problem.
A relationship with a psychopath—living in fear, in chaos, in survival mode.
A relationship with absence—so lonely, even a scream would have felt like connection. But there was no scream. Just silence.
A relationship with abuse—where the fear didn't end even after the violence did.
A relationship with betrayal—where your sense of reality gets shattered. Because everything seemed so perfect... and still, it was a lie.

After that kind of shit... it's not just a wound. It's a psychological landmine.
It's post-trauma.
It doesn't disappear just because you finally meet a good man.
It doesn't vanish in his arms.
It doesn't melt with his concern.

It comes back *right when* you think you're finally safe.
Because that's when the body says: Be careful. This is familiar.

But now I know.
I know how to recognize that voice.

I know when it's my demons—*not* him.
I know it's not his gesture that scares me, but the echo of someone else's hand.
I know it's not his love that hurts, but the scar that hasn't fully healed.

And maybe that's why now… I can pause.
Close my eyes.
And say to myself:

That was then.
This is now.
That was *him*.
This is *us*.
That was survival.
This is peace.

This is me—now.
With new awareness.
With a love that doesn't hurt.
With someone who doesn't trigger panic, but reminds me: you can put it down now.

And PTSD?
It doesn't have to be the end.
It can be proof that you went through something truly hard.
And you're still here.
And you can still love.

It's not weakness.
It's strength.
Not loud. But real.

Author's Note
If you're scared of the good—it's not because you're broken.
It's because you've lived through hell.
And bodies that survived hell… don't trust heaven right away.

๖ CHOOSE A MAN WHOSE TOUCH HOLDS A SOUL

C hoose a man who is tender. Loving.
The kind of man who understands you without words—through touch.
The one who awakens passion in you—not just in your body, but in your soul.
The one who, at sunrise, reaches for you first—not his phone.

Whose fingers naturally find yours throughout the day,
whose lips graze your forehead when he gently tucks a strand of hair behind your ear.
Choose the man who greets the morning sun by watching the light settle on your sleepy face.
Love the man who knows that tears are not weakness.
Who falls apart sometimes—but doesn't hide it.
Who understands that softness is also strength.

It's his sensitivity that sets your soul on fire.
Marry the man who isn't afraid to hold you when the storm comes.
Who holds you so tight that your fear dissolves.
Let yourself be loved by the one who kisses your imperfections.
Who touches your tenderness with care.
Who tends to your sharp edges.
Who warms your scars with the palms of his hands.

Choose the one whose hands make you feel safe.
Wherever life takes you—his touch will always feel like coming home.

Pick the man who, after a hard day, lies down next to you on the grass and looks up at the stars.
The one who gets lost in the peace of your eyes.
Be with the man who lets you dive deep into the ocean of his heart.
Live your life beside a man who is free, wild, and brave—
a man who breaks the mold and doesn't care what's "appropriate,"
only what's *real*.

Marry the man who loves and respects you—
but also respects people and the world.
The one who tears down walls, crosses lines, and faces storms—
just to reach your heart.
The kind of man who's not afraid of his emotions—
and wants to know the real you.

Marry the man who knows he holds both masculine and feminine energy—
and that only the alchemy between them creates something truly powerful.
The one who honors both his strength and his softness.
Who isn't afraid to grow.
To evolve.
To become.

Love the man who touches your soul with care
and takes full responsibility for his words and actions.
The one who can put aside his ego—just to see you smile.
Marry the man who will never try to dim your light.
The one who knows that when you shine—he shines too.

Let yourself be touched by a man who feels *honored* to hold you—
and also wise enough to know when to let go,
so you don't lose yourself in his arms.

Choose the one whose heart has already been shattered once—
but still wants to help you heal.
The one who offers you his own tenderness,
not as a weakness, but as a gift.

I'd marry a man who knows that to truly *touch* a woman—
he must first reach the depths of her soul.
The one who moves to the rhythm of her heartbeat.
Who draws her closer without ever laying a hand on her.
The one whose touch makes her forget how to breathe—
because it's full of presence, care, and quiet love.

And most importantly—
Marry the man who knows how to *touch himself*.
The one who understands:
true love for another begins with love for oneself.

The man who knows his woman is a queen—
and treats her like one.
A man who sees himself as worthy of being your partner.
Who knows how to give—

but also how to receive.

The man whose touch truly holds power—
is the one who knows where, how, and *when* to touch you.
And when he does—
a shiver runs down your spine,
goosebumps race along your neck,
and your senses come undone…

Author's Note:
If he knows how to undress your mind before your body—
that's the kind of man worth taking your dress off for.

🐈 FIRE AND SHADOW

Of a love that doesn't ask — it simply is.

S it down.
Have some coffee.
Or wine.
Tonight I'll tell you about a love that doesn't look like an ad.
It doesn't smell like roses.

But it has something you can feel with every cell in your body —
like fire and shadow.

Do you know that feeling?
When someone walks into your life like a storm.
Doesn't ask if your afternoon's free.
Doesn't care if you're ready.
He just enters.
Looks at you.
And says:

**"I don't want to keep missing you.
I want to be close. Every day."**

And you sit there —
with your tea and a clenched heart —
because the one thing you've been longing for
is suddenly *happening.*

But you're scared as hell.
Not of *him.*
Of *yourself.*

Scared you'll give it all away again.
That you'll drop your life, your city, your people, your work —
only to end up holding a handful of emptiness again.

Scared of that girl inside you
who once loved to the point of self-destruction.
Scared of how ready you are — again.

Because you've already loved once,
with a love that was life or death.
And life lost.

But him?
He says:
"If I have to change my life — I'll change it."

Not out of pressure.
Not as a sacrifice.
But out of *choice.*

Because real love isn't about you packing up, adapting, sacrificing.
It's about one of you carrying the light
while the other is still lost in their forest.

Sometimes in a relationship,
one of you has to be the Robert Louis Stevenson —
the one who crosses the world just to be *near.*
The one who doesn't ask *"Is it worth it?"*
but says *"I can't imagine a world without you in it."*

And then you don't have to decide in panic.
You don't have to drop everything.
You don't have to know what next year looks like.

Sometimes, the only thing that matters is this:

Can I hold you when I break?
Can I show up in the morning just to have coffee with you?
Are you close enough so I don't have to miss you all the damn time?

And if the answer is *yes* —
maybe you don't need to do anything else.

Maybe sometimes… you just need to stay.
To *not* run.

Because true love isn't a show.
It's not a flawless dinner date.
Sometimes, it's a ritual on a stone hill.
At solstice.

With a man who looks at you
as if you were his goddess.

And even if that terrifies you —
maybe it's worth staying.

Just to see
if that fire
can really warm your shadow.

Author's Note:
Don't ask if it's too much.
Ask if it's *true.*
Because what's true —
always finds a way to stay.

🐘 80 MILES FOR ONE HOUR

Love at the motorway services.

It wasn't some Instagram date.
It wasn't a Saturday night dinner by candlelight.
It wasn't a weekend in a spa.
It was one hour.
At a motorway services stop.

The sun was blazing — like it wanted to bless that moment.
No plan.

No booking.
No makeup or clothes for a "special occasion."

Just —
"Hey, maybe we could meet?"
And so we drove.
He from his side.
Me from mine.
Eighty miles.

Just to see each other.
For one hour.

There wasn't a perfect backdrop.
There were coffee machines, people milling about, cars humming in the lot.
But when I saw him — the world just… quieted.

Because in moments like this, it's not about the setup.
It's about the choice.
The fact that you *want* to drive.
That you *care*.
That no one's forcing you — you *just want to be there.*

Some would call it stupid.
Too far.
Not worth it.

For me, it was the best hour of the week.
Maybe of the month.

Because love isn't some grand gesture thrown on social media.
Love is this:
Driving 80 miles to drink coffee from a paper cup
with a man whose face calms your soul.

Not asking *"Is it worth it?"*
Just saying *"I'm coming."*

And don't anyone fucking tell me that a woman shouldn't be the one to make the first move.

Yes, you fucking should.
If you feel it's real —
you show up.
You drive.
You go just to see his eyes,
even if only for a minute.

You *live* that love.
Not sit around waiting for it to sort itself out.

It was a spontaneous thing.
An hour.
A car park.
And a heartbeat racing faster than usual.

I don't measure our closeness in days spent together.
I measure it in *what we're willing to do*
just to stand next to each other for a second.

It's not always about "having the time."
Sometimes,
you just have to **make the fucking time.**

Because those brief, imperfect, unfiltered moments —
they're the ones that *matter.*
They're the ones that stay.
They're the ones that heal.
They're the ones that build the *forever.*

Author's Note:
If you think that was too much —
you've probably never been loved like that.

🐒 LET IT CLICK.
JUST LET IT CLICK.

I'm not asking for much.
Honestly.
I don't need grand declarations on bended knee.
I don't need rings, weekly roses, or spa weekends.

I just want it to **click**.

Between *him* and *them*.

Between *my daughters* and *him*.
Between *him* and *my world*.

Because I already know I love him.
I already know I want to build something with him.

But it's not just my call to make.
It's their world too.
Their hearts.
Their fears.
Their memories.

I don't want them to miss what's most important about him —
that tenderness,
that protectiveness,
that grounding certainty that *I am loved*.

And yes, I'm scared.
Because I know how people judge by the cover.
Because I know you can be wrong.
Because life has told me "no" more times than I can count.

But this time…
I want it to say "yes."

I want them to see what I see.
To know I'm safe with him.
That when I say *"I'm going away with him for the weekend,"*
they don't have to worry.
That they can trust me.
And trust him too.

But also…
I want him to accept them.

He doesn't have to love them like his own.
I'm not expecting miracles.
I'm not trying to force some perfect patchwork family.

I just want him to be as real with them
as he is with me.

No stiffness.
No performance.
No silent evaluations.

Just ease.
Respect.
Openness.

I don't want a repeat of the past.
I don't want a man who sees my children as a complication.
I don't want them to feel like strangers in their own home — ever again.

I want it to click.

And now…
now, I finally *feel* it.

Because this is the first time I feel it like this.

Not like infatuation.
Not like obsession.
Not like the desperate need to belong to someone.

This is different.
Deeper.
Calmer.
Softer.

I *want* this.
I *can* do this.
This is actually happening.

And that's why I care so damn much.

Because I don't want to fuck it up.
I don't want it to fall apart again.
I don't want another tragedy.

Because this time — it's not just *another time*.
This is the *first* time
I actually believe
I might be happy.

Truly.
No conditions.
No *but*s.

Author's Note:
If you've never sat with your heart in your throat hoping your kids see what you see in someone —
congrats.
Some of us are out here trying to make love work... with witnesses.

🐒 IS THERE STILL ROOM FOR ME IN HIS WORLD?

Sometimes I feel like my demons are just waiting —
waiting for me to blink,
to slow down,
to feel too good,

to finally feel safe.
Because that's when they come back.

Just like they did now.

Krzysztof was telling me about the big contracts on the horizon.
Photos worth half a million pounds.
Budgets.
Prestige.
The dream unfolding right before him.

And then — that thought.
That sharp, intrusive voice:

What if there's no room for me when it all happens?
What if, once he has everything he ever dreamed of —
he won't need me anymore?

Because I'm not saving him.
I'm not feeding him.
I'm not mothering him.

And that's what life had always taught me to do.

I was the one who held it all together.
The one who worried about the bills.
The kids.
The future.
I was the foundation. The safety net. The fallback plan.

And suddenly I'm with someone…
who doesn't need saving.

Someone who is the foundation.
Who builds his own world.
Who doesn't need me to fix anything —
he just *wants* me beside him.

And that's where the fear kicks in.

Can I be with a man
who doesn't *need* me,
but just simply *loves* me?

Can I find a place in a world
that doesn't require me to prove my worth
by patching the broken things?

That's the moment.
The one no one talks about.

The moment when a woman with scars doesn't run back —
but pauses.

Remembers the old patterns.
Wonders if she fits.
Wonders if she's *enough*.

I talked to Krzysztof.
I asked him, straight out:

*If you achieve all the things you dreamed of — will there still be room
for me?*

And he didn't even blink.

He said,
You'll always be first.
*If I had to choose between you and those contracts, I wouldn't even
have to think about it.*
Because you matter more.
Because you're mine.
Because you're everything.

And that was the moment
my demons stepped back.

Because I finally understood —
I'm not in his life *for something.*

I'm in his life
because he loves me.

And that's the only thing that matters.

Author's Note:
Crazy how you can spend your whole life fixing other people…

and then suddenly someone just wants to *hold* you —
exactly as you are.
Wild concept.

🐾 MAYBE... THE WHITE DRESS

I never planned to get married again.
Didn't believe in that stuff anymore.
After that one wedding —
thirty-five years ago —
I told myself it had been a mistake.

That marriage was a cage.
That it was for the naïve.
That no one would ever lock me up again
with a ring on my finger.

That I'd never go there again.

And so I lived.
Relationship after relationship.
Man after man.
No plans.
No weddings.
No dresses.

Just life.
Sometimes love.
More often disappointment.

But never... *never* did it even cross my mind
that I might want it again.

Until yesterday.

We were sitting together on that little bench,
in our little cottage,
at the edge of the world.

Surrounded by hills and fields,
and fog settling like feathers into the valleys.

The silence was so deep
I could hear my own heartbeat.
And his breath.

His arm beside me.
Warmth.
Stillness.
Safety.

And then,
out of nowhere,
this thought —
uninvited, surprising:

"Fuck... I think I'd marry him."

I don't even know where it came from.
I don't make plans like that.

I'm not one of those women
who've had their wedding day planned
since high school.

I don't believe in fairy tales.

And yet —
in that one quiet moment —
I believed.

I pictured myself in a white dress.

Not from a catalog.
Something real.
Something mine.

I saw him standing across from me.
And I wasn't afraid.
I wasn't running.

I *wanted* it.

Not for the photos.
Not for the ring.
Not for the name.

Just for that one moment —
when I'd look into his eyes…
and *know*.

That for the first time in my life,
I didn't need to be strong.
I could be a wife.

Because I was loved.

Not *despite* everything.
Not *for* something.

Just loved.
As I am.

Author's Note:

Jesus. I really just imagined a white dress.
Next thing you know, I'll be picking out table decorations.
Someone stop me.

🐝 YOU DON'T HAVE TO HOLD HER BACK WITH FORCE

You don't have to lock her down to make her stay.
You don't need to promise her stars,
swear empty oaths,
or pretend to be someone you're not.
You just need to be real.
And present.

She's not waiting for a prince from some fairytale.
She doesn't need a hero from a romance movie.
She's waiting for a man
who won't walk away when her light fades.

A man who stays quiet when she goes quiet.
Who sees the tears before they fall,
and wipes them away with the sleeve of his hoodie.

Who doesn't ask, *"What's wrong?"*
but simply pulls her close and whispers, *"I'm here."*

She doesn't need grand words.
Just the kind that are true.

Because a thousand "I love you"s
don't mean a damn thing
if they aren't backed by care,
attention,
and actual presence.

You can tell her she's beautiful every day—
but she'll still feel alone
if you don't notice she's worn the same sweatshirt for a week
because grief has drained the will out of her.

She's not the kind of woman who stays for compliments.
She stays for action.
For the small, everyday things.

Like making her tea
when she's too tired to move.

Like texting her when she goes quiet,
just to ask, *"Are you okay?"*

Like not hiding behind work, ego, or pride,
but simply saying, *"I don't know what to say,
but I want to be here with you."*

A woman doesn't leave because she's no longer loved.
She leaves when she stops *feeling* loved.

When she grows lonelier
lying next to someone
than she ever did sleeping alone.

When she has to pretend for too long
that everything's fine.

When being strong
becomes her only survival skill—
and no one sees that her strength
is just a cover for exhaustion.

She doesn't walk away from a man.
She walks away from a place
where her soul can no longer breathe.

So if you love her—
be the place she wants to return to.

Don't test her loyalty.
Don't push her limits.
She doesn't need another war.

She needs rest.
Peace.
The certainty
that she doesn't have to keep proving
she's worth your time.

If you can't be present
when her world is falling apart—
you don't deserve to stand in her light
when it's glowing.

You'll hold onto her
not when you promise her the world,
but when she no longer has to ask herself:
"Is he really here?"

You'll keep her
when she no longer fears
you'll disappear without a word.

You'll keep her
when she's finally able to put down her armor
and not fear being hurt
in her nakedness—
not of body,
but of soul.

Let your arms be her refuge,
not her prison.

Let your words heal,
not harm.

Let your actions weigh more
than all the grand gestures combined.

Love her like every day is your last.
Respect her like her heart
is the only treasure you'll ever own.

And above all—
be honest.
Even when it's hard.

Because for a real woman,
truth weighs more
than a thousand sweet little lies.

You don't have to force her to stay.
You just have to show her
that by your side,
she doesn't have to fight.

That with you...
she can finally rest.

Author's Note:
And if you're not ready for that—
do us both a favor
and don't even knock on the damn door.

🐚 LOVE DOESN'T LIVE IN CAGES

You can't force someone to love.
You can't keep a person close just because you crave them.
Because the moment you try to "have" someone — you stop seeing them.
Love doesn't live in conditions.
It doesn't breathe inside expectations.
It doesn't bloom where there is pressure.

If I have to be the way you want me to be in order to be loved —
that's not love.
That's a contract. A transaction. A performance tailored to
someone else's taste, hoping to be chosen.

Love is when you can be fully yourself.
With the messy parts. With the soft parts. With the fears and the
wounds.
With all that's not yet healed.
And still — you are loved.

I don't need someone to control me so I don't drift away.
I need someone who can hold space — so I can fly.
I need freedom.

Not because I want to leave.
But because that's the only way I can truly stay.

There's no greater gift than saying:
"You don't have to. But if you want to — stay."

I don't want a relationship built on fear.
Fear that I'll leave. Fear masked as jealousy. Fear that clips my
wings to keep me grounded.
Because if you have to hold someone back — it's no longer love.
It's a cage.

And love… love is freedom.

It's a choice. Every single day.

It's the fact that I could be anywhere —
but I choose to be here.
With you.

Author's Note:
Don't try to "keep" anyone.
Don't convince, beg, or manipulate.
If someone feels free and stays anyway — that's love.
Anything else is a prison with good branding.

?❧ AND WHEN YOU'RE NOT HERE

We can't always be together.
There's not always time to talk.
There aren't always words.
There are days when life pulls us in different directions.
His job. My writing. Responsibilities, children, everything at once.
Days that move fast, without mercy.

And yet — he's there.

Not with grand gestures.
Not like some cinematic hero.
But like someone who knows that presence isn't measured in hours of conversation — it's measured by presence itself.

Before I even open my eyes, he calls.
4:35 a.m.
On the way to work.
From his car. From the dark before the dawn.

He calls just to say "good morning."
To hear my sleepy voice.
To be with me — before everything starts.

And in that moment, I know I'm not alone.
That someone, before starting his own day, thinks of me.
That for someone, I'm the first thought of the morning.

Sometimes, there's no time to talk.
But then I get a heart emoji on WhatsApp.
A "thinking of you."
A little kiss.

It's not about the message.
It's about what it means.

It's as if that tiny sign is saying:
"I'm here. I haven't disappeared. I'm thinking. I miss you. I'm holding space for you."

Sometimes he calls just for a minute.
A few seconds.
Just to see my face.
He says nothing.
He doesn't have to.

There are moments when we just look at each other through the screen, and silence is enough.
Silence that holds everything.
Silence that whispers, "You're not alone."

During the day — short messages.
Simple ones.
Sometimes just a word.
Sometimes just a sentence.

But each one is proof.
Proof that I'm present in his world.
That I'm in his thoughts — somewhere between a photo shoot and the next appointment.
Between a breath and a glance.

And that... that's what matters.

Love doesn't come from the grand things.
Not from candlelit dinners.
Not from movie-scene kisses.
Not from perfume-scented letters.

Love is made of the small things.
A message at four in the morning.
A random phone call that comforts more than a thousand words.
A heart when you thought you were forgotten.
A minute of screen-time silence that says, "I'm right here."

That's what builds the real stuff.
The truth.
The thing that stays.

Because in all those little things... I am seen.
And I know that to someone — I really matter.

Author's Note:
Maybe that's what true intimacy is — not when you *have* time, but when you *find* a second to say: "You mean something to me."

ও SHE'S NOT LOOKING FOR A SAVIOR.

She's Looking for Presence.

She's not looking for a man to rescue her.
She's rescued herself too many times
for anyone to ever truly know the whole story.

She's walked through storms
that should've broken her.
She's survived nights

where her own crying was the only sound in the room.
And still—she got up every morning.
No applause.
No witnesses.
No pats on the back.

She doesn't need a hero.
She doesn't need someone to fix her.

She's already done the inner work.
Healed the wounds
that were too heavy to carry.
Learned to stand on her own feet
even when the ground beneath her shook.

She's not looking for someone to save her.
She's looking for someone who *shows up*.

Someone who is *there*.
Not just when things are good.
Not just when it's easy.
Not just when loving her feels effortless.

Looking for her?
Then don't play the disappearing act.
Don't flinch at her strength.
Don't run
when she stops smiling.

She's not chasing fireworks.
She wants quiet, honest presence
on an ordinary Monday afternoon.

She wants a man who listens
without trying to fix her.
Who understands
that her independence isn't a wall—
it's proof
she's survived more than you'll ever know.

She wants a man who *stays*.

Even when she's tired,
wary,
sharp-edged.

Someone who chooses her every day—
not out of duty,
but from the heart.

Someone who sees her as a whole woman.
Not a project.
Not a plan.
Not a rescue mission.

She's not asking for a fairytale.
She's not asking for a prince.
She's not asking for drama.

She just wants to be seen.
Heard.
Supported.

To love—
and be loved.
For real.

And if you ever meet a woman like her—
don't ask, *"What can I do for you?"*

Just *be there*.
Stay when leaving would be easier.
And love her
when she forgets she deserves to be loved.

Author's Note:
And if you're not ready for that—
don't confuse her healing with an invitation
to start over from scratch.

෨ THE STONE CIRCLE — WHERE SOULS COME HOME

S it down.
Seriously.
Make yourself some tea. Or wine.
Take a deep breath.
Because today, I want to tell you something that goes beyond

logic.
Beyond falling in love.
Beyond anything you've ever felt.

This wasn't a date.
It was a ritual.

There were no candles.
No dinner for two.
No rings, no kneeling, no grand words.

And yet—
everything in me knew:
this was a soul vow.

In that sacred place, surrounded by ancient stones,
our energies did something I still don't know how to name.

We touched the same stone.
And for that one moment—
time dissolved.

The world went silent.
The past disappeared.
The future didn't matter.

There was only this:
me and him.

Or rather—
our souls, seeing each other again.

I don't know what it was.
There are no words for it.
But I know this:
it was real.

There was no fear in me.
No noise.
Just stillness.
The kind you feel when, after years of wandering,
you finally come *home*.

Not a place.
Not a person.
A home *in yourself*.

One you don't have to decorate.
One you don't have to explain.
You just *know*:
This is it.

That's exactly how I felt.
Like a child curled into its mother.
Like a woman who, for the first time in her life,
doesn't have to perform to be wanted.
Like a soul that knows:
no one will ever pull her away again.

There were no butterflies.
No thrill.
Just peace.

The kind that says:
You're safe now.
You don't have to run anymore.
You don't have to fight.
You don't have to prove you're worthy of love.

Because he already knows.

He held me.
So damn tight.

But not with possession.
With something else—
like holding someone who just came back from war.
As if saying:
Don't go back there.
You're home now.
I've got you.
You're safe.

And I believed him.

With every cell.
Every scar.
Every memory.

In that moment,
every trauma went still.

This wasn't infatuation.
This wasn't love as I knew it.

It was more.
Something that needs no words.
No declarations.
No noise.

It felt like we were one body.
One soul.
Like someone had split us long ago—
and we had finally found each other again.

And no,
this wasn't a fairy tale.
Not a movie.
It was real.
It happened.
In a stone circle.
In this world.

I feel him inside me.
Every breath.
Every touch.
Every glance.

Like I'm learning him for the first time,
and remembering him from always.

Like we simply came back to each other.

And I'm not afraid of my demons anymore.
I know they'll return.
They always do.

But they won't destroy me.
Because someone now holds me
like no one ever has.

And I know—
if needed, he would flip the world upside down for me.
He'd cross oceans.
He *knows* that what we have isn't a romance.
It's not a relationship.
It's not a phase.

It's something you *feel*.
Something that breaks every mold.

And if you're reading this thinking,
God, I want to feel that too—
I'll tell you this:

It's real.

But it doesn't come when you're searching.
It comes when you're ready
to stop being afraid.

When you're ready
to let your soul find its way.

Author's Note:
Not everyone gets to stand in a stone circle and feel their soul
finally exhale.
But if you ever do—
don't doubt it.
Don't run.
Just… stay.

🐍 I WOKE UP AFTER KUPALA NIGHT

A nd nothing was the same.
It wasn't a typical date.
No wine.

No candles.
No clichés.

There was silence.
The kind you can finally breathe in.

There was space.
Real space.
There was a place.
Ludwell, Wiltshire.

On the map—nothing special.
But for us—Ground Zero.

That's where it happened.
Something that changed everything.

It was only our second time seeing each other—
but our first *real* date.

The first time the energy started shaping into something bigger.
Before that, there had only been coffee.
A long conversation.
Words.

But on that day—there was more.

*We met on the morning of June 22.
Which means...
I woke up after *Kupala Night*.

The holiest Slavic night.
The solstice.
The longest day of the year.
The time of fire and water.
Of lovers.
Of sacred union between masculine and feminine.

A time of rituals—
even when you don't fully understand them,
your body and soul know something is happening.

And that day—

we were called.

I didn't know it was a ritual yet.
But it had already begun.

Our bodies knew.
Our souls recognized each other.

And the land… remembered.

We brought signs with us:
I brought **Feather and Fire**.
He brought **Stone and Silk**.

Air.
Fire.
Earth.
Water.

Four elements.

Only one was missing:
Spirit.
The fifth element.
The one that unites the rest.

And a month later—
Spirit answered.

Exactly one month later,
under an almost full Moon,
in the *very same fields*,

a crop circle appeared.

Not some random swirl.
Not a farmer's prank.
Not chaos.

A pentagram.
Perfectly inscribed in a circle.
Five arms.
Five elements: earth, water, fire, air, spirit.

A symbol of harmony.
Of balance.
Of the human as microcosm—
with head and four limbs woven into the cosmos.

But also the symbol of Venus.

Because Venus—the planet of love—
draws a pentagram in the sky
as it traces its orbit through divine geometry.

She governs beauty, desire, magnetism…
and everything that passed between us.

As if the Earth whispered:
*"I saw you.
And I marked it down."*

Beside the pentagram—
three arcs.
Like arms embracing the space.
As if to say:
*"What happened here was sacred.
It stays."*

And nearby—three smaller circles.
Three points.
Three energies.
Or maybe…
you, him, and what exists between you.

Everything in perfect harmony.
As if sky and earth together had sealed your meeting.

Because sometimes, the Universe whispers.
But sometimes—
it draws a pentagram in the wheat
and watches to see
if you'll notice.

We noticed.

Because this wasn't a fairy tale.
It was a myth
carved into the world itself.

We met after Kupala Night—
when everything holds the most power.

We brought the elements.
The Earth gave the sign.
Venus sealed it.

And maybe—
that wasn't the end of a ritual.
Maybe—
it was only the first sign.

Author's Note:
If that's what *coincidence* looks like—
I want more of these miracles.

---

*We met on the morning of June 22.
Which means...
I woke up after **Kupala Night** (*Slavic midsummer festival held on the shortest night of the year — a mystical celebration of fire, water, love, and sacred union between masculine and feminine forces*).

❧ LOVE THAT SOOTHES THE NERVOUS SYSTEM

It doesn't start like in the movies.
There are no fireworks, no spectacular wow.
There is silence.Peace.
Warmth.
And that astonishing relief that… nothing hurts.

Because when a man is gentle with you — not just in touch, but in tone, in gaze, in his presence — something inside you starts to melt.

Your body, which has worn armor for years, suddenly begins to breathe.
You don't flinch at every message.
You don't brace for disappointment.
You don't prepare for anything — you just are.

Because he doesn't trigger your anxiety.
He soothes it.

That's what emotional safety does.
You can't fake it.
You can't force it.
Either you feel safe being yourself — or you're still performing.
And I didn't want to perform anymore.

I had built an entire empire of defense mechanisms.
Smiles when I wanted to cry.
Silence when I wanted to scream.
Forgiveness when I should have walked away.
Pretending to be strong when I was fragile like a cracked eggshell inside.

And then someone appears who doesn't push.
Doesn't interrupt. Doesn't judge.
Just stays.
With tenderness.
With patience.
With presence.

And that's when the real transformation begins.
Not the kind the world sees.
The kind that happens under the skin.
In quiet moments.
In breaths that no longer stay shallow.
In arms that don't ask questions — they just hold.

This isn't just a relationship.
This is healing.
It's the slow re-learning of trust.
It's disarming the minefield in your head.
It's realizing you're not hard to love —
you were just loved badly for too long.

He doesn't have to do grand things.
Sometimes it's enough that he speaks to me in a calm voice.
That he looks at me with attention, like he truly sees.
That he asks, "Are you okay?" and stays, even when I say I'm not.

It's those little things that teach my body it doesn't need to run.
Not gestures from a romantic comedy.
Acts of presence.
Stitching me together again, one quiet day at a time.

That's why some women glow when they're loved right.
Not because they got a new man.
Because they finally stopped being afraid.

Because someone loved them without trying to change them.
Without dimming their emotions.
Without conditions.

Someone heard their story — and didn't walk away.
Someone saw their scars — and didn't flinch.
Someone heard their tears — and stayed.

And it was enough
for the soul to rest.
Not in euphoria.
Not in drama.
In a quiet "I'm here."
In a steady "right now."
In a safe "together."

Because this is the love that heals.
Not loud. Not flashy.
But real.

Steady.
Soothing.

The kind of love where I don't have to be anyone else.
Because finally —
I am loved without fear.

Author's Note
No, he didn't slay any dragons.
He just showed up and stayed — and for once, that was enough.

🐾 UNDRESS ME FROM SILENCE

D on't slowly unbutton my shirt.
Don't slip your hand beneath my dress, reaching all the way to my stomach.
Don't tear off my lingerie, or pull me out of sweaters too thick for this season—
but perfectly tailored to fit my fear.
Undress something else.

Undress me from silence.
Unfasten the half-spoken truths
I button up too carefully each morning,

like the last clasp of a well-behaved girl's dress.

Pull shame from over my head.
Slide fear from my hips.
Take off the tension from my legs—always ready to run.
Strip restraint from my hands.
And self-censorship from my lips.

Undress all of that.
Take your time.
Don't touch just to open me.
Touch me so I stop being afraid.

Lay me down.
But don't strip away the light.
Don't leave me naked and alone.
Wrap me in certainty.
Not in words—but in presence.
In a warmth I don't have to question.
In an arm that stays even when I fall silent.

Lie beside me for a long time.
Longer than I ever learned to believe someone could.
Until I stop waiting for you to vanish.

I will tell you, again and again,
that everyone leaves.
That it's dangerous to trust.
That touch is never safe.

And you—
you don't need to answer.
Just stay.

Have patience with my fears.
With the part of me that still doesn't know
love can stay.
That not everything has to hurt.
That being undressed can also be sacred.

Don't take me.

Receive me.

Author's Note:
The deepest kind of undressing doesn't begin with taking off her clothes—
but with taking off her fear.

🐿 HOW TO TRUST WHEN YOUR MIND REPLAYS OLD PROGRAMS

I t's not that I don't trust him.
I DO trust him.
And I love him.
And I feel with every cell in my body that this is it.

Not a lie.
Not some smooth-talking guy from an app.
Not a fleeting crush.
This is what I once thought didn't exist.
And that's exactly when the shit show begins.

Because then *he* shows up.
That little gremlin in my head.
The one who sits on my shoulder and pulls the strings,
launching old files in my brain named:
"WARNING – YOU'VE BEEN THROUGH THIS BEFORE"
"CAREFUL – THIS WILL END LIKE THE OTHERS"
"REMEMBER HOW IT TURNED OUT?"

And you know it makes no sense.
Because this is different.
Because he is *not* one of *them*.
He doesn't feed off you.
He doesn't want to move in after three dates.
He's not looking for a mother or a wallet.

He wants to build.
To give.
To stay close.

And still... the brain does its thing.
Without asking your heart.
Without listening to your soul, which is screaming:
"Trust him. You finally can."

It's not, for fuck's sake, that you don't trust *him*.
It's that you don't trust *yourself*.

Because you've been wrong so many times.
You've handed your heart to people with filthy hands.
You've ended up in ruins, in therapy, in pieces.

So now, when someone good, real, mature shows up —
it's not that you don't believe *him*.
You just don't know if you can believe *you*.

If you won't mess it up again.
If you won't slip into old patterns.
If you can love without betraying yourself.

And that's the worst kind of fear —
when you're afraid that maybe you're no longer capable
of loving normally.
That every gesture will be filtered through trauma.
That every plan will be a risk assessment.

But maybe… this is the moment
to tell that gremlin on your shoulder:
"Shut the hell up. I know what I'm doing."

Maybe it's time to risk it.
Not because *he* promised.
But because *you* already know it's real.

And even if it ends in pain —
at least this time,
it won't hurt because you betrayed yourself.

Author's Note

Yes, my head's loud. But my soul is louder. And right now? She's
not running. She's staying.

🐾THE TRAUMA
OF GRATITUDE

I don't know how to receive.
Even when someone gives me something out of love — I still
scan it for danger.
What does he want in return?
What will he expect?
Will he throw it back in my face later?
Will he take it away the moment I let my guard down?

Instead of feeling grateful — I tense up.
Instead of joy — I feel fear.
Because I don't fucking know how to *take*.
Not without guilt. Not without overthinking.

All my life, I had to *earn* everything.

Love? Only when I was "good."
Closeness? Only if I wasn't "too much."
Help? If I promised to repay it — with interest.
Care? When I didn't complain. When I didn't disturb.
When I didn't need too much. When I wasn't a burden.

So now, when he brings me tea in bed,
instead of saying *thank you*, I think:
"I need to do something for him too."

When he says he loves me and wants to be there for me,
instead of smiling, I think:
**"Why? What does he see in me? I'm complicated. This won't
last."**

Gratitude trauma.
That's probably what it is.
That fucked-up compulsion to *repay*.
The inability to receive kindness without guilt.
Because someone once taught me that gratitude is a *debt*.
And debts must be paid.
Preferably with interest. Preferably immediately.
Otherwise, you're just an ungrateful bitch who doesn't
appreciate a damn thing.

So even when he says:
"I want to take care of you."
Something inside me clenches.
Because somewhere in the back of my head, that voice whispers:
"Be careful. Nothing is ever really free."

And I know — this isn't about him.
It's about *me*.

My scared, scarred inner world that doesn't believe
you can be loved — just like that.
Without conditions.
Without earning it.
Without paying for it with some version of perfection.

But I want to learn.
I want to learn how to *receive*.
Gently.
Without flinching.
Without calculating.
Without trying to be extra good in return.

Because isn't that what love is supposed to be?
Not a contract. Not a transaction.
Love isn't: *"I give, so I get."*
It's: *"I give because I want to. Because I see you. Because you matter."*

So maybe today — I'll try.
I'll take the cup of tea.
With a soft smile.
No debt. No guilt.
Just... receive it.

Because maybe, just maybe...
I do deserve it.

Author's Note:
Healing starts with a sip of tea you didn't make yourself — and
didn't feel bad for accepting.

🐿 THAT PLACE BETWEEN HIS SHOULDER AND NECK

It's not just touch.
Not just his hands on my skin.
Not just closeness.
It's an explosion.
A silence pulsing with warmth.
It's permission—to be fully myself.
Unguarded. Exposed. Hungry.

I have my place.
Between his shoulder and his neck.
That hollow curve of the body that knows my breath.
That cradles my face like something sacred.
That whispers without words: *you belong here.*

When I rest against him,
the world disappears.
I'm no longer a mother. No longer the strong one.
No longer the woman who has to carry everything.

I'm just me.
Breathing. Pulsing.
In his arms.

Every touch of his is a language only my body speaks.
We don't need words.
All it takes is his fingers tracing my skin.
Along the curve of my hips. The inside of my arm. The back of
my neck.
And I'm ready to open.
Not just my body—but all of me.

This isn't just desire.
It's hunger.
So deep, it aches sometimes.

Sometimes one touch is enough.

A brush across my back. A squeeze of the hand.
And I know—he knows me.
He knows my skin. My soul.
Every wave. Every tension.

We can't not touch.
It's a physical impossibility.
As if our bodies have their own hearts.
And they only beat when they're together.

When we make love…
It's not sex.
It's a journey.
It's stepping into another dimension.
As if our bodies want to melt into each other.
To stop being *him* and *me*.
And become only *us*.

In that moment, I exist only for him.
And he, only for me.
Nothing else exists.

No one's ever touched me like that.
No one's ever caressed me with such devotion.
No one's ever kissed me like he does—
like he knows every lifetime I've lived before,
like he's kissing every wound, every fear, every "I'm not enough."

This isn't just passion.
It's surrender.
It's closing my eyes and falling into something larger than both
of us.
Deeper. Truer.

And you know what's most unbelievable?
He's not my type.
Wouldn't have been.
If he walked past me on the street—I wouldn't have noticed him.

But when I saw his eyes in that photo…

Time stopped.
Because I already knew those eyes.
It wasn't infatuation. It was recognition.

As if my soul said: *Finally.*

And now…
my body knows only him.
And wants nothing else.
Because with him…
I am whole.

Author's Note

Funny, isn't it?
That I used to think love should look a certain way.
That passion had a checklist. That desire came in a specific package.

And then he touched me.
And everything I thought I knew… unraveled.

Now I know.
The right touch doesn't ask for permission.
It simply *finds you.*
And you melt—because it feels like home.

Even if it comes in a body you never expected.

🐚 HOLD ME

Hold me.
Not because it's polite.
Hold me because sometimes, it's the only language my heart remembers
when words refuse to come.
Hold me when you see me go quiet —
that's when I need you most.
Hold me when I laugh —
because joy shared with you tastes different.
Hold me after an ordinary day — the kind with no story —
so I know that even the quiet can feel safe when you're near.

Hold me when I'm tired.
Don't ask what happened.
Just stay.
Hold me when I come back from a war with the world —
even if you can't see the wounds.

Hold me when I'm falling asleep.
And before I even open my eyes.
Because that's when I know: I don't have to *do* anything —
I just have to *be*.

Hold me when I piss you off.
Before either of us says something we'll regret.
Hold me after everything —
after the tears, after the kisses, after the silence.
Because it says more than words ever could.

Hold me on the street,
in the store,
around people —
just so the world knows I'm yours.

Hold me,
because your arms are the home I once dreamed up
and didn't believe could exist.

And even though I pretend to be strong,
sometimes I ache for someone to simply hold me.
Hold me even when you don't understand.
Even when you don't have the words.
Because there are moments when I don't need a solution.
I just need *you*.

Close.
Still.
Here.

Author's Note:
Sometimes, the safest place on Earth is a quiet hug from the one

who sees you — even in silence.

DON'T ASK IF I'LL BE OKAY. JUST STAY.

D on't ask if I can handle it.
Don't ask if I need anything.
Don't ask if I'm doing fine.
Because I'll smile.
I'll say I've got this.
That I'm fine.
That it's nothing.
That I can manage.

But it's not true.

It's just my autopilot. My survival mode.
Because too many times, when I said "I need something,"
I heard silence.
Or an empty promise.
Or I was laughed at.
Ignored.
Disappointed.

So I stopped asking.
I learned to carry it all on my own —
the bills, the kids, the pain, the disappointments,
the lonely evenings, the heartbreaks,
the hopes that eventually died.

And no, I'm not proud of that.
But I am made of it.

I'm the woman who rescues.
Who puts on gloves and cleans up other people's messes.
Who doesn't flinch at blood, or tears, or truth.

But that doesn't mean I don't want to be rescued sometimes.
Because I do.
I want to fall apart —
for a moment.
For an hour.
For a whole weekend.

Without being judged.
Without being asked.
Without being told I'm too much.

I want you to see it before I say it.
To respond before I ask.
To hold me before I break.
To make me tea before I even sigh.

I want you to *be there.*
Really be there.

Not with words,
but with your presence.

It's not that I can't ask.
It's that I never had anyone to ask.

So if I'm letting you close now —
don't screw it up.
Don't make me regret it.
Don't make me put my armor back on.

Just stay.
No speeches.
No solutions.
No strategy.

And show me that even strong women...
have the right to rest.

Sometimes I wonder
if men even understand
what it really means
to be with a strong woman.

Not one who pretends to be tough.
But one who had to be.
Because life gave her no other choice.
The one who raised her kids with no support.
Who held it all together
even when her own world was collapsing.

You don't have to worship her.
You don't have to put her on a pedestal.

Just *see her.*
See her tiredness behind that smile.
See the story behind the strength.
See the cost she paid for surviving.

And if you're a man
who meets a woman like that —
don't ask if she needs anything.

Because she won't say it.

Offer.
Act.
Do something.

Not because she's weak.
But because no one ever did.

And if you don't know how —
just sit beside her.
Take her hand.
Be silent with her.

And show her
you don't have to be a hero.

Just don't disappear.

Author's Note:
Sometimes love isn't about knowing what to say. It's about staying long enough to matter.

EMOTIONAL WITHDRAWAL SYNDROME.

When you're scared... because nothing hurts anymore.

I don't know if it's peace.
Or relief.
Or just... numbness.
I meet someone, and everything is good.
There's conversation.
There's tenderness.
There's understanding.

And there he is — a man who doesn't disappear,
doesn't play games,
doesn't test me.

And you know what?
I start to panic.

Not because of him.
Not because of *us*.
I'm afraid because...
I don't feel *anything*.

There are no fireworks.
No emotional bomb after the first glance.
No heart punch.
No adrenaline, no panic, no "will he text me?"

There's just peace.

So much peace that I start to wonder
if I'm still capable of feeling.

Because I've lived my whole life in survival mode.
Fight or flight.
That's all I knew.
Always ready.
Always with a backup plan.
Always holding an emotional sword,
armor tight on my chest.

And now… I don't know what to do with that peace.
Because I don't know how to live
without that little voice in my head screaming,
"Something's about to blow up."

And now everything is… good.
And that "good" scares the shit out of me.

It feels like I'm coming off a drug.
Like I swallowed a handful of sedatives.
Or smoked too much weed.
Everything works. Everything's fine.
But I don't feel the highs.
No lows.
No chaos.

And that terrifies me more than anything I've ever known.

It's called *emotional withdrawal syndrome*.
Yeah. That's a thing.
After toxic relationships.
After constant tension.
After the kind of love that meant adrenaline + anxiety + longing.
Suddenly… there's silence.

And you have no idea what to do with it.

Because silence used to mean punishment.
Silence meant *you messed up*.
But now?
Silence is just… silence.

And I have to learn to breathe in it.

Instead of "I love you so much it hurts" —
it's "I feel safe with you."

Instead of "if he leaves, I won't survive" —
it's "even if he leaves, I'll still be whole."

Instead of "I miss you so much it crushes my lungs" —
it's "I'm happy you're here,

but I don't fall apart when you're not."

And that's when you start to panic.
Because you don't recognize this state.
You don't know how to just *be in it.*

Because you were addicted to intensity.
To highs.
To chaos.

And now... there's nothing to fight.
No fire to put out.
No game to decode.

You feel like an addict in detox.

But maybe that's when real love begins.
Not the one that gets you high —
the one that makes you *whole.*

This calm doesn't mean you feel nothing.
It means you're no longer afraid.
Your body is no longer in a state of war.

You can take off your armor.
Lay down your sword.

And even if this feeling lasts a week, a month,
a year, ten years —
you know it's worth it.

Because now you know what love feels like
when it doesn't hurt.

This isn't lack of emotion.
It's emotional sobriety.
The kind you've never known.
The kind you have to work for.
The kind you first want to reject...
before you fall in love with it.

And maybe that's what real maturity is:
Not throwing yourself into emotional tornadoes

just because they're loud.

But choosing to stay
where it's quiet.
And safe.

Even if your demons are bored to death in the silence.

Author's Note:
If your heart is still searching for chaos,
maybe peace isn't boring.
Maybe it's just unfamiliar.
Give it a minute.

੨੭THE WOUND
OF REJECTION

She's a bitch. Shows up uninvited and never really leaves.

She lives in your throat when someone takes too long to reply.
She crawls under your skin when you notice you're being seen...
less than you are.
And she screams inside:
You're not enough. Again.
He didn't have to hit you.
He didn't have to yell.
All it took was silence.

Eye rolls.
Comparisons.
Being there in body, but never in presence.
Always disappearing
when you needed to be seen
the most.

So you start adjusting.
Softening.
Shrinking.
Changing your tone, your words, your shape, your opinions —
just to be chosen.

And still... he pulls away.
Goes quiet.
Fades out.

And you're left clinging to nothing.
And hating yourself for still trying.

Because no one ever told you
that *you* weren't the problem.

That some men simply can't *see*.

Men who feel too small beside your truth,
too dull beside your mind,
too weak beside your strength.

And the only way they know how to survive
is by shrinking you down
until they don't feel like losers.

But *you*
are the one left thinking
you're broken.
That you need fixing.
That you're "too much" of something —
or not enough of everything else.

And that's when the second wound shows up.
The wound of *adapting*.

Fuck, that one burns.

You start losing yourself
just to never be rejected again.

But here's the truth:
You can be soft, smart, loyal and devoted.
You can cook, suck his dick,
quote his favorite movie.

You can understand him, support him,
endure the silence.

You can do *everything right*
— and he'll still leave.

Or worse:
he'll stay... and you'll still feel alone.

Because the wound of rejection
was never about you.
It was about the kind of man
you ended up with.

To one man, you'll always be *too much*:
Too loud. Too independent. Too ambitious.

To another — *not enough*:
Too emotional. Too free. Too intense.

And no matter how much you bend
like a fucking yoga master,
you'll never be "just right."

Too much.
Too little.
Too soon.
Too late.
Too deep.
Too shallow.

But then...
there's a different kind of man.

One who doesn't want to take anything from you.
Doesn't want to change you.
Doesn't want to convince you
to feel less, talk less, want less.

He just wants *you*.

All of you.
With your story.
With your feelings.
With your past.

And for the first time in your life,
you don't have to *try*.

You don't have to tense up,
shrink down,
play small.

You just... exist.

Because he doesn't heal that wound
with pretty words.

He heals it
by receiving you.

All of you.

No edits.
No conditions.
No performance.

Author's Note:
Some wounds don't need fixing.
They just need to be seen
—and held.

﹩WHAT IF I'M JUST A BODY?

This isn't a letter to you. It's a letter to myself.
But maybe one day you'll read it.
And understand what trembled inside me.

Because everything is good.
Better than good.
I can feel you.
Your hands. Your attention.

Your eyes peeling back every layer I ever hid.
But suddenly...
that familiar voice returns.
Quiet, but persistent.
Whispering:
"What if that's all there is?
What if you're just a body to him?"

And again, I start to feel the fear.
Not of it fading.
But of there being nothing underneath it.
Of this whole thing vanishing the moment desire cools.

Because I've been here before.
Too many times.

I've been the body.

The thing to be wanted.
Held at night.
Left in the morning.

I've been everything that can be touched
—but nothing that gets seen.

They didn't ask about my soul.
Didn't want to know her.
Didn't care what I felt,
what scared me,
what made me ache.

They cared about how I looked.
How I moved.
How I tasted.

Not how I go silent when I hurt.
Not how I cry at night when no one sees.

And so now, when *you* are here —
fully, completely, truly —
I find myself scared again.

Because if that passion ever fades,
if sex stops being fire...
will you still be here?

Will you stay
when I no longer smell like morning coffee and sin?

When I stop being your wonder
and start being just... me?
Exhausted.
No makeup.
Head full of chaos.

Will you still see me then?

Will you still want me —
the *me* that is lived,
not the one that is touched?

I *know* you're not like the others.
I know you *see*.
But my demons don't read facts.
They only read history.
And sometimes... they come back.

So if one day I pull away,
if I start to disappear —
don't take it personally.

It's not you.
It's the echo.
The echo of not being seen.

It's not doubt in you.
It's memory.

But I'm writing this
because I want to believe this ends here.

That with you —
I'm whole.

That if the fire quiets,

we'll still be here.

Not because there's no sex.
But because there's everything else.

I want you to know
that I'm learning, too.

Learning how to be loved —
differently.

Author's Note:
Love that stays after the fire fades
is the only love worth trusting.

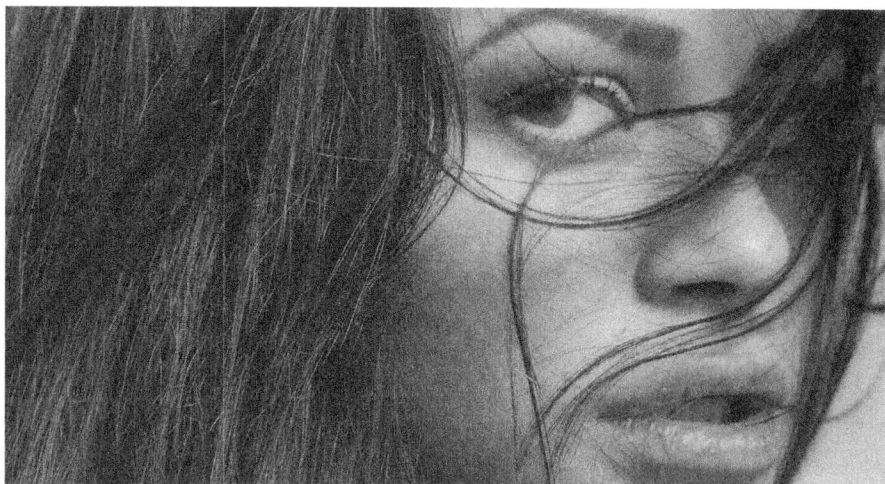

THE ART OF RECEIVING

We've spent our whole lives giving.
Caring.
Holding it all together.
Always with a list in our heads.
Responsibility on our backs.
And the quiet belief that if we don't do it — everything will fall apart.
Being a giver becomes part of your blood.

Your hands.
Your breath.
Your automatic *"It's fine, I've got it."*
Even when you don't.

And then one day,
life — or love — or a man — wants to give something *to you.*
Not for something.
Not in return.
Just because.

And suddenly there's resistance.
Fear.
Shame.

How come?
I'm supposed to just... *take it?*
Without proving my worth?
Without guilt?
Without instantly saying, *"I'll get it next time"?*

Even when a man offers you something from his heart —
a dinner, a gift, a moment of rest, a weekend away —
your first thought isn't *thank you.*
It's:
"Do I really deserve this?"

Because we were raised to give.
But no one taught us how to receive.

No one taught us that it's okay to *just take it.*
That we don't have to explain ourselves.
That we don't have to repay it with the exact same value.
That accepting doesn't make us *less.*

But it's hard.
God, it's hard.

Because the voices in your head start screaming:
"If he gives you something, he'll expect something back."
"Don't take too much — you'll seem entitled."

"You're not worth that."

But here's the truth —
receiving is an act of love too.

You let someone see you.
Care for you.
Offer you a piece of themselves.

And in return,
you say: *I trust you.*

So I'm learning.
Step by step.

That it's okay to take.
That I'm not only here to carry.
That I don't have to control everything.

And that sometimes,
the bravest thing a woman can do —
is simply open her hands.

Author's Note:
Receiving without guilt is a revolution in a woman's nervous system.

❧TRUTHS
THAT STAY

You know what?
I don't chase people anymore.
I don't drag anyone along who wants to leave.
Because if someone is truly *mine* —
they'll stay anyway.
I don't need to fight for them.
I don't need to bend, explain, apologize for feeling too much.

The right people don't need explanations.
And the rest won't understand anyway.

And if someone feels pulled elsewhere —
then go.
The door's wide open.
Let them find what they couldn't find with me.

Because if you have to hold someone back by force —
they're already gone.

And I'm done giving away parts of myself in small change.
I'm not an emotional ATM.
I'm not free therapy.

Besides...
love can change a person in a second.
But heartbreak?
It dismantles them even faster.

You can see it in their eyes.
Eyes always tell you who's never coming back.
Some people leave a relationship —
and never return, even if they're still around.

And still...
where someone is truly waiting for you —
you'll always arrive right on time.
You won't be late.
You won't miss it.
Because you *can't* be late for what was meant to be yours.

And if life hurts?
Then it hurts.

But fuck it —
I won't let anyone convince me that suffering is the point.
It's not a mission.
It's not some holy rite of passage.
It's just a temporary state.

And living in constant pain?

That's a luxury I can't afford anymore.

I don't have time to play the victim.
I don't have the strength to be brave 24/7.
And I don't have to.

There are people...
who were born to walk through life alone.
Not because there's something wrong with them —
but because they're built differently.
They feel differently.
They love differently.

It's not good or bad.
It just *is*.

And I had to accept that too.

What you're searching for —
is also searching for you.
But it won't find you curled up in the corner of your own wounds
waiting for someone to fix you.

You've got to get up.
You've got to show up.
You've got to be brave —
even with shaking hands.

And you know what?

Sometimes life separates two people
just so they can finally realize how much they mean to each
other.

But sometimes...
it separates them forever.
And you have to survive that too.
You have to swallow it whole.

What happened once may never happen again.
But if it does —
if it returns —

then it will come back a third time.
It always does.
Because life has its patterns.
You just have to learn how to read them.

And if it hurts now —
if everything's falling apart —
then it's not the end yet.

Because everything ends well.
And if it didn't end well —
then it simply isn't the end.

Author's Note:
We stop chasing when we finally understand: what's truly ours
will never need convincing.

THE ONE WHO HEARS MY SOUL

The greatest gift
life can give you
is not someone who hears your words —
but someone who feels them.
Someone who senses the truth hidden between the lines,
who catches the trembling that others miss,
who reads the pauses louder than the sentences.

Someone who — no matter what —
will always find time for you.
No matter the hour.
No matter the place.
Not because they have to.
But because they want to be where you are.

A person like that is rare.

Because they don't just listen —
they make you feel important.
Like your thoughts matter.
Like your words are a home someone truly wants to stay in.

But you know what's even more beautiful?

When you meet someone
who doesn't need words to hear you.
Because they hear your soul.

No sound.
No letters.
No translation.

They feel what you haven't yet found the courage to say.
They see what you try to hide.
They know your thoughts before you can name them.
And they share your emotions —
even when you stay silent.

That kind of bond might seem unreal.
But when it happens —
it asks for nothing.

No explanations.
No justifications.
No fight to be understood.

Because your souls
speak in a language
no one else understands —
and no one ever has to.

It's *your* language.
Your connection.
Your truth.

Author's Note:
Some people don't hear your voice.
They hear your soul — and answer with silence that feels like home.

❧ SHE ISN'T HARD TO LOVE

She's not difficult.
She's just tired of almosts.
She's not asking for miracles.
Not looking for a fairytale.
She simply has a soul from another era —
a time when love wasn't rushed,
when touch mattered more than likes.

Her heart beats slower.
Softer.
Deeper.
Longing for tenderness.
For presence that doesn't shout,
but stays.

She believes in slow mornings,
handwritten notes,
forehead kisses.
Late-night talks under the stars.
Fingers laced together.
A cup of honey tea,
made without asking —
because someone noticed
she's had a rough day.

And if you're ever lucky enough
to be loved by her —
you'll see she doesn't want the world.
She just wants closeness.

To be part of your days —
but also your dreams.
To know you think of her
even when she's not around.

These aren't demands.
They're the ways she feels safe.
Seen.
Loved.

Because that's how she loves —
through little things.
A warm towel after a shower.
The car started on a cold morning.
Her favorite tea, waiting.

Not because she asked.
But because you *wanted* to be that man.

She doesn't want to be your project.
She doesn't want to be rescued.
She just wants to be *seen*.
Present in your everyday.
In your language of love.
In your future.

She's been the one who stayed
when others walked away.
The one too often overlooked.
The one who waited too long
to be loved fully —
not just when it was easy.

That's why now,
she clings to the kind of love
that's quiet,
but sure.
The kind that doesn't promise the moon,
but shows up —
especially when everything else falls apart.

She dreams of notes on the fridge.
Of your hand running through her hair.
Of hearing *"I'm not going anywhere"* —
and, for once,
someone actually meaning it.

Because to her...
Love isn't words.
It's gestures.
Presence.
Gentleness that heals
what others broke.

And if you ever meet a woman like her —
don't let the world convince you
she's asking for too much.

She's only asking for something *real*.

For effort.
For consistency.
For a love unafraid of the ordinary.

And in return...
You'll get a kind of devotion
this world has almost forgotten.

Author's Note:
She's not too much.
She's just enough — for a man who's not afraid to show up.

🐦 THERE'S NO WAY
TO TELL THIS STORY

If you asked me,
"So, how was it?"
I wouldn't know how to answer.
Not really.
What am I supposed to say?
That it was beautiful?
That he was wonderful?

That the wine tasted different,
and the candlelight danced like it knew the rhythm of my
heartbeat?

That doesn't come close.
It doesn't capture any of it.

It wasn't dinner.
It wasn't sex.
It wasn't just another man,
another evening,
another attempt at closeness.

It was...
presence.

As if someone suddenly turned off the whole world —
all the past disappointments,
all the questions,
all the defenses I'd spent years building.

It was like a prayer without words.
Like a touch that didn't ask, didn't take, didn't judge —
just *was.*

Like silence —
not empty,
but *full.*

Full of safety.

When he said he loved me,
I had no doubt.
Not because it sounded nice.
But because I felt it
in every inch of my skin.

It wasn't something to *hear.*
It was something to *know* —
deep beneath the ribs.

And all of it happened there,

in a fairytale cottage hidden on a hillside,
forgotten by the world
but chosen by fate.

Before us stretched a view
too surreal for words —
a sea of green,
rolling fields,
valleys and soft hills,
with trees and sky melting at the edge.

No people.
Only sheep and lambs bleating in the distance,
like they were mocking our peace with laughter —
then even they went quiet.

There was silence.
But not the cold, empty kind.
The kind you could *sink into*.
The kind you could lay your soul down in
and just… rest.

His whisper in that silence
sounded like a vow.
And my laughter didn't have to be quiet —
because there was no one to judge.

And in the morning…
the fog had settled in the valleys,
like someone had tucked the world in
under a white blanket.

I stared out the window
and couldn't look away.
It wasn't a view.
It was a *painting*.
One that stays behind your eyelids for years.

And I thought to myself:
If anything could be called *home* —

it was that.

One evening.
One night.
But it felt like we'd always been there.
Like our souls had been waiting
for that place,
that moment,
that single *I love you* —
which wasn't a declaration,
but a recognition:
"I found you. I see you. I feel you. You're here."

I don't know what comes next.
But I know this —
that night changed everything.

Because it wasn't a night with a man.
It was a night with love.
The kind that doesn't need to shout —
because its breath beside you
is enough.

Author's Note:
If it feels like home after one night — maybe it's not the first time
your souls have met.

🐾 LOVE THAT REMEMBERS

There comes a moment
when true love no longer shouts.
It doesn't slam doors.
It doesn't ride in on a white horse
or sparkle with gold.
It simply… arrives.
Quietly.

Gently.
Like a whisper in the dark.
Like candlelight among the ruins
of your former relationships.

And suddenly you *know* —
it all made sense.
Every fall.
Every "almost."
Every sleepless night
with your heart left outside your chest.

Because *this* was where it was always heading.
This version of you
was the one it was meant to fall for.
Not the one pretending.
Not the one chasing fairytales.
But the one who walked through fire.

This is not a love story.
Not a fling from an app.
This is love made for a queen.
For the woman who no longer begs.
For the one who remembers herself from centuries ago.
Who walked through lives, wars, bodies, and worlds,
carrying within her the memory of that one soul.

He — or she —
may not look the way you imagined.
They won't arrive in fireworks.
They won't win you with words.
But they'll look at you.

And your soul will tremble.
Because you'll know them.
Not with your eyes.
Not with your body.
But with your whole being.

It'll be someone who knows your wounds.

Who was there when you received them.
Who remembers your deaths
and your rebirths.
Who knows you —
not from *this* life,
but from *all* your lives.

And you'll feel it.
In every cell.
In every breath.

This won't be love that needs saving.
It won't be something to fix.
It will already be *whole*.
Something divine.

And memory will return.
You'll start to remember who you really are.
Why you're here,
now,
in this body.

You'll feel it in a touch.
In the tremble of a voice.
In a look that dissolves
every defense you've ever built.

Because this is not a love of this world.
It's soul love.
The kind that knows you
better than you know yourself.
The kind that never needs to change you —
because it sees you already whole.

And even if the world says it makes no sense,
even if logic screams *this won't work* —
your heart will know.
Your body will know.
Your soul will know.

Don't run.
Because it's speaking to you now.
The love of your soul.
Your other half.
The one who remembers.
The one who's returned.

Maybe not today.
But when it comes —
you'll recognize it.

And you'll understand
that everything — absolutely everything —
that came before
was just the path
leading you back to it.
To that one space where fear no longer lives.

Only love.
Love that remembers.

Author's Note:
If it feels ancient and eternal at once —
you're not dreaming.
You're remembering.

🐚 I SEE YOU

He didn't say I love you.
He said: I see you.
And it meant more than any confession.
It was the embrace of a soul.
Like in *Avatar*,
when Neytiri looked at Jake
and didn't just see a man in a Na'vi body —
she saw his essence.
Who he was beneath the skin,

beneath the story,
beneath the armor.
His pain.
His fight.
His loneliness.
His courage.

And she acknowledged it all.
Without pity.
Without needing to change it.
With a love that doesn't scream — but sees.

How many times in life have we felt invisible?
Wearing a smile like a mask.
Saying "I'm fine"
when everything inside was falling apart.
Falling asleep next to someone
who knew our body but not our soul.
Looking in the mirror
and wondering if anyone would ever truly see us again.

Until one day...
someone looks.

Not *through* you.
Not *at* you.
But *into* you.

And suddenly — everything quiets.
It's not falling in love with eyes,
or hips,
or laughter.
It's falling in love with what the world doesn't see.
With what's left after the storms.
With what cracked — but still shines.

"I see you" is more than words.
It's presence.
It's stillness.
It's saying:

I know who you are.
And I'm not leaving.

Because only someone who once felt invisible
knows how much that hurts.
Only someone who's searched for a gaze
that says "you matter"
can look at you like that.

And when that kind of love arrives...
there are no loud declarations.
Just silence that heals.
A touch that doesn't take — it receives.
Eyes that don't pierce — they hold.

It's a love that doesn't need you
to become a better version of yourself.
Because it already sees
everything you are.

And then,
you no longer have to perform.
You don't have to fear saying too little,
doing too much,
or falling apart at the wrong time.

Because you are *seen*.
Completely.
And that's enough.

Because once you've been seen —
truly seen —
you'll never go back
to those who only looked.

Author's Note:
When someone sees your soul and stays —
that's not chemistry.
That's recognition.

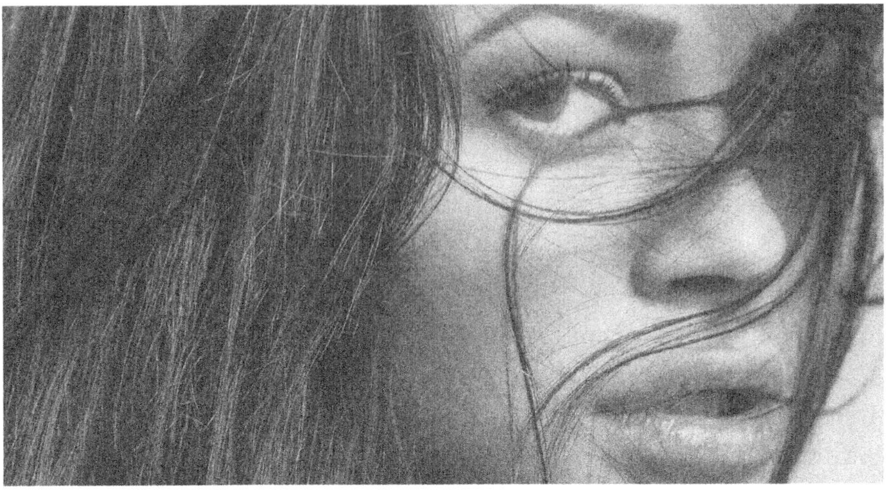

❧ THE RITUAL UNDER THE FULL MOON. A NIGHT THAT WASN'T ORDINARY

It was a Full Moon in Capricorn.
Not a coincidence.
Not just in the sky —
but inside me.
A full moon that carried
the weight of decisions.
The kind of energy that stops you from lying to yourself.
That forces you to look in the mirror
and say the truth.

Not the truth about what you want.
But about what you already know.

That evening,
we returned to our cottage.
The place that had already become
a sanctuary of silence, closeness, and truth.

But that night...
something shifted.
Something trembled in the universe,
as if someone had pressed *play*
on a script written long before we ever met.

And the ritual began.
Unplanned.
But written.

It wasn't just sex.
Not even just an act of love.
It was something greater.
Deeper.
Quieter than words —
louder than a scream of ecstasy.

Every touch was a seal.
Every kiss — a vow.

Every whisper — a spell.

It wasn't about desire,
though it burned.
It was about something more.

In that one night,
we sealed more than just our bodies.

We sealed a choice.
I chose him.
He chose me.

No drama.
No words.
Just the silence of a body that knows the soul.

Under the Full Moon in Capricorn —
the sign of commitment, maturity, and structure —
we chose not to run anymore.
Not to pretend.
Not to hide behind the past.

It was sex that healed.
Love that vowed.
A night etched into every cell of my body.

And when I opened my eyes in the morning,
I knew.
I was no longer the same woman.

Because that night...
we didn't just make love.

We made a vow.

No words.
No witnesses.
Only the Moon as our seal.
And the soul — that remembered.

Author's Note:

Some vows are not spoken.
They're written in the silence between heartbeats.

🐦 SEX IS THE BODY.

LOVE IS EVERYTHING.

To have sex,
all you need is one night.
To truly love...
one lifetime is not enough.

Sex caresses your skin.
Love touches your mind.
And reaches your soul.

Sex can be nice, exciting, passionate —
but it's just the hallway.
Love is the temple.

Because sex is physical.
And love…
love is closeness.
Real.
Deep.
The kind that doesn't care about makeup, age, or weight.
The kind that undresses not your body —
but your fears.

Sex demands.
Love gives everything it has —
and more.

Sex is a flame.
Love is the fire that keeps you warm all winter.

Sex is a moment.
Love is the home you return to every day —
even when everything else has fallen apart.

Sex can be a craving.
Love is a choice.

Sex is earthly.
Love is divine.

Sex leaves you naked.
Love wraps you in the feeling of being wanted.
Seen.
Chosen.

Sex is hollow without feeling behind it.
Love…
fills every wound, every emptiness,

every breath.

Sex is for those afraid to feel.
Because in sex, you can pretend.
In love — you're truly naked.

Love isn't a scene from a romantic movie.
It's the choice of everyday.
It's looking into my eyes when it hurts.
It's understanding me when I'm silent.
It's the hand that doesn't ask — just holds.
It's presence that doesn't demand — just is.

Sex is an adventure.
Love is magic.
Madness.
And miracle.

Not everyone who sleeps with you
wants to love you.
But the one who loves you —
never stops desiring you.

And that changes everything.

Because it's not about what you do in bed.
It's about what remains
when you get out of it.

Author's Note:
You can undress for anyone.
But only one person will ever see you truly bare.

🪝 DANCE IN
THE RAIN

It's not that the storm comes
because you did something wrong.
It comes because life
doesn't need your permission.
It wrecks everything —
without asking,
without warning,
without mercy.

And you're left standing
in the middle of the rubble,
holding questions
no one will ever answer.

You wait.
You think if you just stay still,
if you don't breathe too loud,
it might pass you by.

But it doesn't.

It tears through you from the inside.
It shreds your peace
into scraps.

You cling to the old life.
Because it's the only one you've ever known.

All those
"you should've been somewhere else",
"you should've been someone else",
"this wasn't how it was supposed to go."

And you stumble.
Over your own disappointments.
Over illusions.
Over the people who didn't stay.
Over the hope you kept hidden
in your pocket for dark days —
and this is the day.
But it doesn't work.

You start to cry.
But these aren't soft tears anymore.

This is the soul howling.
These are tears that know
something inside you is ending.

That you won't go back
to how it was.

That you have to fall apart completely —
until there's nothing left
but naked truth.

And then...

Right then,
sitting on the metaphorical floor of life —
messy, smudged, swollen-eyed from too much hope —
something inside you stops being afraid.

Not because it doesn't hurt anymore.
But because it hurts
for so long
you stop fighting it.

And you learn.

Not how to rebuild what was.
But how to breathe
with what's left.

You learn to dance.

Not on a stage.
Not in the spotlight.
Not to applause.

But in the rain.
With heavy boots.
With a heart that no longer believes in fairy tales —
but believes in itself.

Because you understand this:
peace doesn't come
when the storm ends.

Peace comes
when you're no longer afraid of it.

When you say,
"You can pour down —
but I'm going to dance anyway."

Not for the world.
For yourself.

Because now you know —
not every wound
has to heal quietly.

Some stay with you forever.

But you learn to live with them.
Not as a victim.
But as a woman
who walked through hell —
and didn't lose herself.

Author's Note:
You weren't made to survive the storm.
You were made to become the thunder.

🐾 YOU STAYED
LIKE A TATTOO

W e didn't love carefully.
This wasn't the kind of love you find in brochures —
the safe kind,
the peaceful kind,
the kind with rules and balance.
It was force.
A storm.
A love that leaves a mark.

And it did.
You stayed.

Not just beside me —
but inside me.

You stayed like a tattoo.

Deep.
Permanent.
Unwashable.
Unforgettable.

In Loreen's song she sings,
"I don't wanna go, but baby we both know… this is not our time."
But I don't want to go.

Because I feel,
with every cell in me,
that this is our time.

I don't want to disappear.
I don't want to run —
not from myself,
and not from you.

I want to stay.
I want to be.
I want to breathe
with you.

I don't know what comes next.
But I know this:

If love stays like a tattoo —
then I want to wear it with pride.

No hiding.
No shame.
No regret.

Because if someone's going to be etched
into me forever —

let it be you.

Author's Note:
Some loves don't fade.
They ink your soul.
And that's exactly where I want you.

🐾 NOT NOW...
BUT ONE DAY.
AND ALWAYS.

Sometimes love doesn't begin when we want it to.
Not when everything falls into place.
Not when we feel ready.
Sometimes love arrives...
too early.

Or too late.

But always right on time.

When I met you,
everything in me said *yes* —
only life hadn't caught up yet.

The days were too short.
The distance too long.
Deadlines, children, responsibilities —
everything shouting: *not yet.*

But the heart doesn't wear a watch.

The heart just knows.
And I know.

Because sometimes, love means just that: waiting.
Not giving up.
Not surrendering.

But showing up. Quietly.
Every day.
In thoughts.
In hope.

In the choice to stay —
even if, for now, it's from afar.

Because loving you
isn't only about being close.
It's about believing — even when I can't touch you.
It's about closing my eyes and knowing you're there.
It's about falling asleep with your name on my lips —
without fear.

Because I know you're out there.
And I know I still exist in you.

Real love doesn't need constant proof.
It doesn't shout.

It trusts.

It waits.
It *knows.*

I believe everything happens
when it's meant to.

And if we are real —
life will catch up.
The universe will clear a path.
Love will find time.

Because not every story starts with *now.*
Some need more courage.
More patience.
More truth.

But I know this much:

We already found each other.

The rest...
is only a matter of time.

Author's Note:
Real love doesn't rush.
It remembers.
And it stays — even before it begins.

🐦 THE MARK THAT WON'T WASH OFF

S ome wounds don't bruise.
There's no blood.
No stitches.
No cast.
And only you know something broke.

Because some pain doesn't live in the body.
It lives in the soul.

On the outside, everything looks normal.
A smile.
Work.
Kids dropped off at school.

But inside — a hole.
Not fresh.
Not dramatic.
Just... empty.

A mark.
Not from someone.
But from *something.*

Something you lived through.
Or something you never received.

From that night.
That conversation.
That look.

From the words that never should've been said.
Or the ones that never were.

We carry those marks inside us.

Like tattoos we never chose.
Like scars made from silent blows.
Like burned-in symbols that whisper:
You were there.
You survived.
You were changed.

And you will never be the same woman again.

But you know what?
Some of those marks...
are sacred.

Proof that you lived.
That you felt — to the edge of pain.
That you loved — beyond your limits.

That you made it through.

Don't try to erase them.
Don't cover them with makeup, smiles, or perfection.

They are yours.
They are real.

A mark on the soul isn't a weakness.
It's proof that you have one.

Author's Note:
Don't be ashamed of your scars.
They're just your soul's way of saying: *"I was here. And I felt everything."*

🐦 THE FACELESS WOMAN

Some of us were born remembering who we were.
Others spent years searching for their true name –
lost somewhere between others' expectations,
roles we were forced to play,
and masks that clung so tightly to our skin
we forgot they weren't our own.
The faceless woman is not weak.
She is the one who survived in the shadows.
The one who endured.

Because sometimes, to survive,
you had to become someone else.
The girl who doesn't cry.
The woman who stays silent.
The one who says, "I'm fine,"
while screaming on the inside.

That wasn't weakness –
it was strategy.
But every strategy has its price.

One day, you wake up
with a face that isn't yours.
A voice you don't recognize.
A life that doesn't smell like you.

The faceless woman begins in emptiness.
She doesn't know who she is—
but she knows she can't pretend anymore.

Something cracks.
Something stirs.
And though it's terrifying,
this is when real magic begins.

Sometimes all it takes is a single mirror.
A single candle lit in the dark.
A single word spoken for the first time without fear.

The work that follows is not easy.
Peeling off the masks hurts—
especially the ones we wore to stay safe.

Those masks were often never ours.
They were gifts from mothers, fathers, lovers, teachers.
They were spells made of other people's expectations.

But each mask that falls leaves a mark.
And that mark can become a rune.
A scar of power.
A symbol of strength.

The true face returns slowly.
A glance caught only at night.
A whisper that speaks the truth when the world is silent.
An identity that cannot be named—
because it's not fully human.
Because it comes from somewhere else.

The faceless woman remembers
she was always something more.
That she carries inside her
something no one can name.

Something wild.
Something primal.
Something untamed.

This is not a story of collapse.
This is a story of awakening.

Because once all the layers are stripped away,
only the core remains.
The essence.
You.

Sometimes fierce.
Sometimes gentle.
Always real.
Always one of a kind.

They don't teach this in school.
It's not in fairy tales.
Because a real woman has no single face.
And that's exactly why—she holds them all.

If you feel that you are her,
know this:
you don't need ready-made answers.

Sit in silence.
Light a candle.
Ask the question.

And don't run
when the answer comes.

Truth can be terrifying.
But truth sets you free.
And freedom—
is the beginning of magic.

Author's Note:
She's not broken.
She's returning to herself.

🐚 WHEN SOULS TOUCH

Making love… it's not just a physical act.
It's not a performance or a spectacle of passion.
It's a sacred space – intimate, almost mystical – where two souls meet beyond words, beyond movement, beyond skin.
It's not just sex. It's not fleeting desire.
It's a return.
To yourself. To another. To something far greater than the body.

True intimacy doesn't begin in bed.
It begins earlier – in a gaze that doesn't judge, but sees.
In a hand that doesn't demand, but listens.
In a conversation where no masks are needed.
It begins when you stop fearing that you're "too much." When you let yourself truly feel – with your whole body, your whole being.
When the body is no longer an object… but a gateway.
A gateway to the soul.

Because real lovemaking… is a spiritual ceremony.

It's the moment when you undress not just your body – but your shame, your tension, your old survival patterns.
And suddenly… you're there.
Real. Alive. Seen.

There's something sacred in the moment a woman lets her shoulders drop.
When she allows someone to touch her skin as if they're touching her soul.
When every movement whispers: *"I don't want to take you. I want to feel you."*

It's not about perfection. It's not about how you look tangled in sheets.
It's about the energy you bring – the space between your breaths.
It's about the silence between kisses being louder than the cries of pleasure.

When it's true, you don't need a script.
You don't need lingerie from a catalogue or moves from a movie.
You just need to *be*.
Fully.
With softness. With trembling. With all your chaos and light.

He doesn't come to fix you.
You don't come to impress.
You meet… to meet.

Because true lovemaking is the reunion of souls that remember each other from before this lifetime.
It's a deep *"I see you"* – not through the eyes, but through recognition.

When he kisses you, he doesn't just kiss your lips.
He kisses your story.
Your wounds.
Your *"I don't believe in love anymore."*
And for the first time in a long time... you believe it *might* be different.

Your bodies are only instruments.
But they play an ancient song – the song of return.
Where there is no dominance.
No power struggle.
Only surrender.

Because when you make love *truly*, the world goes quiet.
There is no time. No *what if*.
There is only now – holy, heated, trembling.
There is only the soul that says: *"I'm here. All of me. I'm not leaving."*

And when he looks at you with such stillness that your breath catches –
it's not because he wants you.
It's because he *feels* you.
And you – for the first time in your life – feel *yourself*.

Author's Note:
If you've ever felt that sex was something to *give*, *prove*, or *perform*...
Know this: that was never love. That was the lie.
Real closeness doesn't take. It doesn't hurt.
It heals.
And you'll never confuse it with anything else again.

🐒 THE MICHELANGELO EFFECT

(How it feels when someone doesn't try to remake you – but sees who you truly are)

Y ou know, for most of my life, I thought love meant someone trying to change you.
Like love was a never-ending list of demands:
"Speak softer."

"Don't overreact."
"You care too much."
"Stop being so dramatic."
And then someone came along
who didn't want to change a damn thing.

He looked at me—and he *saw*.
Not a project to fix.
Not a mess to clean up.
Not a version to polish.

Just... me.
The raw me.
A little cracked, a little bent.
But whole.

And it hit me like a punch in the gut.

Because... how?!
No proving?
No smoothing out, smiling more, shrinking to fit?

No.

He looked at me like the deepest part of me—
the part I'd buried under fear and shame and other people's
voices—
was the most beautiful.

As if he already knew
that version of me
I only ever saw in dreams.

And then it clicked.

It's not about finding someone who loves what you've *made* of
yourself.
It's about someone who gently uncovers what was always there.
Hidden.
Muted.
Trapped under everyone else's "should."

That—

that is the Michelangelo Effect.

It's not someone carving you from stone.
It's someone brushing away everything that's not you.
Someone who says:
"You can drop that now.
That's not yours.
Underneath—it's you."

And suddenly...
you start to breathe.

I don't know if he does it consciously.
If it's some magic between souls.
Or just fearless love.

But I know one thing:
Being with him,
I started to grow from the inside out.

I started to write differently.
Feel differently.
Breathe like I finally had permission to exist.

Not because he gave it to me—
but because I stopped denying it to myself.

That part was mine.
But his presence...
was the light that helped me see the path.

And now I know:

Love is not about fixing someone.
Not about patching a woman together to meet someone else's standards.
Love is meeting someone
who sees the whole of you—
even when all you see are the broken pieces.

That's the Michelangelo Effect.
Not a new you.

Just the real you—
finally set free from silence.

Author's Note:

You were never broken.
You were just buried.

🐚 DON'T EARN
IT. JUST BE

Sometimes you look at the man standing in front of you and think:
"This can't be real. There's too much light in him.
Too much beauty—
and it hurts."
But instead of stepping back,
he moves closer.
And he says *you* are the one who's not from this world.

And that's when you want to hide.
Because how can he not see your scars?
Your fears, your broken pieces, your nights
when you held yourself together
with nothing but the clench of your jaw?

But he *does* see.
And still—he doesn't run.
He doesn't try to fix you.
He doesn't try to "deserve" you.

He simply wants to stay.

Not as a hero.
Not to erase your past or drown it in grand gestures.
But to be there—
with his soul wide open,
with a body that doesn't want to dominate,
just hold you.
Without conditions.

And you know what happens then?

Your mind rebels.
Because this was supposed to be harder.
He wasn't supposed to recognize you.
He was supposed to walk away.
He wasn't supposed to handle the intensity.

But he stays.
And the more of yourself you show,
the more he wants to stay.

He says it's an *honor* to know you.
And you think:
"How? How is that possible?
To know me means to know my demons."

But that's exactly what he wants to learn.
Not to tame them.
But to know how to hold you

when they rise to the surface again.

I don't know if anyone can ever truly be ready for that.
But I know this—
I don't need someone trying to "earn" me.
I don't need a perfect man who gets everything right.

I need a human
who doesn't walk away when I'm no longer radiant.
Who stays
when I say again:
"I don't know if I can do this."

Because love doesn't happen *because of.*
It happens *in spite of.*
It happens *anyway.*

And when he looked at me and said simply,
"I'm here"—

I breathed like after a storm.
With relief.
With faith.
With the quiet thought:

"Maybe I'm not from this world.
But maybe… neither is he."

Author's Note:
Let's be honest—half of us would run the moment someone saw us *too well.* We say we want deep love, but the second it shows up and says "I see you," we panic like it's a police raid.
So here's to the ones who stay when you unravel. And to the miracle of not having to apologize for being human.

🐾 LOVE ISN'T A PLAN. IT'S A CHOICE.

And I just made it.

One day, someone asked me:
"What does love mean to you?"
And you know what?

I didn't have to think long.

Because now I know:
Love is a choice.
Not a plan.
Not a guarantee.
Not a contract with the future.

It's the conscious, daily choice
of the person standing right in front of me.

I don't know where this will lead.
I don't know how it ends.
There's no map.
No script.

But I have him.
And I have me.
And I have *this*—
whatever lives between us.

And that's enough.

Because true love doesn't always arrive with logic.
Sometimes it shows up as presence.
As a voice.
As energy.

As silence that soothes you—
instead of scaring you.

As that *something* you feel under your skin,
even when you can't explain it.

I know what some people would say:
"Slow down."
"Think twice."
"This won't end well."

But I'm not choosing this love because I'm naive.
I'm choosing it because it feels like mine.
Because it feels like *me*.

In this womanhood.
In this sensitivity.
In this hope.

Maybe it'll fall apart.
Maybe it won't last.

But if I have to choose—
I choose him.

Not because I'm certain.
But because I *feel* it.

I feel like myself when I talk to him.
I feel like this isn't a fairytale—
but a breath.
I feel like I don't have to pretend.
Like I can love without strategy,
without filters,
without begging for crumbs of affection.

And I feel—
deep in my bones—
that he feels it too.

I don't know what will happen.
But I know this is *real*.
This is *now*.

And even if it doesn't last forever—
it will live in my heart
as the bravest decision I ever made.

Because love isn't always what survives.
Sometimes, it's what *lives*.
And that...
deserves everything.

So today—
with my whole heart—
I choose him.

Author's Note:
Love isn't safe.
But it's the most honest thing I've ever done.

🐿 LOVE BY CHOICE

I love you in the purest kind of freedom.
Not because I need to.
Not because I'm afraid to be alone.
Not because the world says I should "have someone."

I love you because you are the space where I can be fully myself.
No pretending. No shrinking. No masks.

I love you in quiet, gentle moments.
But I also love you in the wild chaos your presence sometimes brings.

In the intensity that can feel overwhelming—yet never pushes me away.
Because it's a part of you.
And I have chosen you—whole.

You are my center when I fall apart.
My anchor when nothing else makes sense.
You're the shoulder I lean into...
and the world I disappear into.

I don't need you.
But I want you.
Not because something is missing,
but because with you—I am whole.
And from that wholeness, I choose to give.

What I feel for you doesn't come from fear.
It's not attachment in disguise.
It's a meeting.
Raw. Sovereign. Intimate.
A soul connection that existed long before our bodies ever touched.

I see you.
In all your versions.
The strong, certain, fearless one.
But also the soft one. The tender one. The part of you you show only to me.

And it's that version I love the most.

I'm not your "other half."
I didn't come to complete you.
I am a whole universe, standing beside you—by choice.

Because my heart knows yours.
Because my body remembers your touch before it ever felt it.
Because my eyes knew it was you—before I could name what I felt.

In your kiss, my fire is reborn.

In your presence, the noise of the world fades.
In your arms, I find a peace that doesn't need words.

This is not a love that cages.
Not a love that demands we fit into someone else's mold.

This is a love that lets us grow.

A love that doesn't close doors—
but opens windows.

A love that says:
"You don't have to prove anything. Just be."

We don't possess each other.
We don't cling.
We don't play roles.

We simply... choose each other.
Every day. Consciously.
With lightness. And courage.

And that's what makes this love so sacred.

Not because it's easy.
But because it's real.

Author's Note:
Not every woman knows how to love in freedom.
And not every man knows how to hold space for her to do so.
But when two people stop performing—
and start *being*—
something unexplainable appears.
A love that doesn't need promises.
Because it *is* the promise.
A home in itself.

🐒 ON THE
OTHER SIDE OF
THE MIRROR

They always called her strong.
But no one ever asked if she had a choice.
She carried it all.
Not because she wanted to — but because no one else would.

The family. The business. The kids. The bills.
Her mother's anxiety. Her father's absence.
Her partners' disappointments.
And her own desires — stuffed deep into a drawer labeled *"maybe one day."*

One day, a man told her:
— You're too independent. It's not feminine.

It stung. Not because he was right.
It stung because, for a moment, she felt like that little girl again
—
the one who had always been told: *"You're too much."*
Too loud. Too smart. Too wild. Too difficult.

That night, she had a dream.
She dreamt of a mirror.

On one side stood the woman everyone saw — strong, capable, composed.
On the other — her Shadow.

Soft. Sensitive. Unsure.
The part of her no one had ever allowed to cry.
The part that had to grow up before she ever got to be a child.

— You are my weakness — she whispered.
— No, — the Shadow replied. — I am the part of you they never let feel.

She woke up with a trembling heart. And for the first time in years — she cried.
Not because she was weak.
But because she finally stopped holding herself together.

A few weeks later, he appeared.

Quiet. Grounded. Attentive.
He didn't try to impress her.
Didn't storm in with grand gestures or heroic promises.
He just… *saw her.*

He noticed the silences between her words.
He didn't try to fix her.
He didn't try to save her.
He said:
— I don't want to rescue you. I want to see you.

She froze.
Because she didn't know how to *be seen.*

She'd always been *useful,* but never *enough.*

They began to talk.
About fathers who disappeared.
About mothers too afraid of their own femininity.
About how they were taught that vulnerability was shameful,
and strength meant dominance.

She learned she didn't need to be *masculine* to be safe.
He learned he didn't need to be *tough* to be a man.

They met each other — on both sides of the mirror.
Not to change.
But to be whole.

She let herself soften.
He let himself feel.

And for the first time — neither of them had to perform.
There were no masks. No battles. No pretending.
Just truth.

One day, during a walk, she stopped, looked into his eyes, and
said:
— Thank you for not fearing my strength.

And he replied:
— Thank you for seeing my softness.

And in that one moment, they both knew — *this* was love.
Not a transaction.
Not a strategy.
Not a roleplay.

But being fully seen — and fully loved.

Author's Note:

Maybe you've had that dream too.
Maybe you've seen yourself in the mirror — soft, tender, raw.
Don't be afraid of her.

She is not your weakness.
She is the gate to your truth.

You don't have to fight anymore.
You don't have to prove anything.
The wholeness you're searching for is already within you.

You just have to stop dividing yourself.

🙝 ACKNOWLEDGEMEN TS

First — to my Grandma.
For being the first person who ever loved me.
Truly.
Unconditionally.
Without "you have to earn it."
Without "be a good girl."
Just... me.
You held me when everything else was falling apart.

You taught me tenderness that doesn't judge.
You showed me how to love with silence, with presence,
with a hand gently reaching out.

You're still within me.
In every word of this book.
Thanks to you, I know that real love doesn't hurt—
it builds.

Thank you to my daughters.
For teaching me every day what it means to be a mother.
Not a perfect one.
But a present one.

For loving me even when I have less patience than I wish I did.
For helping me return to myself—
because of you,
and also *for* you.

Thank you—
to me.
For not giving up halfway.
For hitting rock bottom
and choosing to bounce back.

For enduring every day when all I could think was,
"I can't do this anymore."
For the fact that today—
I can.
Today, I'm still here.
And I'm no longer afraid
to live truthfully.

And finally—thank you, Christopher.

Not for saving me.
I didn't come here to be rescued.
I came as a woman who had already picked up her broken pieces.
But also—
as a woman who still carried fear,

doubt,
mistrust.

A suitcase full of demons that didn't disappear—
they just stayed quiet.

With you, I didn't have to pretend they weren't there.
With you, I could finally face them in the light of day.
And not run.
Not hide.
Not freeze myself.

This book was written day by day—
starting the moment I met you.

It's not just a love story.
It's the story of what happens to a woman
when, for the first time in her life,
she no longer needs to defend herself.

Each chapter isn't only *about us*.
It's about *me*—
the woman who came face to face with her own fear
the moment she realized
she might actually be loved—
for real.

Thank you for not pulling away when I did.
For staying when I wanted to run.
For your patience
when I was guarded, frozen, chaotic.

For not being afraid of me.
Of my strength.
Of my wounds.
Of my demons.

Thank you for being here.
So that, for the first time—
I can be.

Whole.

Safe.
Real.

🐍 STAY IN TOUCH

If this book spoke to you — don't let it be the end of our connection.
You can reach me here:
www.featherandfire.co.uk
info@featherandfire.co.uk

Also by the author:

The Woman Who'd Been Seen

An emotional journey of healing, rage, and rediscovery.
Kindle version available at:
https://www.amazon.co.uk/dp/B0FJSFYJKC

Coming soon
A new four-part fantasy series inspired by Slavic mythology.
Think *Harry Potter* meets ancient rituals, pagan spirits, and the forgotten gods of the land.
First book in progress.

About the author
The author writes straight from the gut — raw, emotional, untamed.
She believes that healing begins the moment we dare to tell the truth.
Even when it's messy. Especially when it's messy.

If this book touched you, please consider leaving a review.
Just a few words on Amazon help this story reach more women who need it.
Thank you for reading.

Printed in Dunstable, United Kingdom